LISTENING WITH SPEAKING

牛津技能世界
英语听说专项训练 1

[英]朱莉·黄◎著　　石若琳◎译

北京科学技术出版社
100 层童书馆

著作权合同登记号 图字：01-2023-5267

图书在版编目（CIP）数据

牛津技能世界. 英语听说专项训练 1 /（英）朱莉·黄著；石若琳译. -- 北京：北京科学技术出版社，2025. -- ISBN 978-7-5714-4473-0

Ⅰ. G624.313

中国国家版本馆 CIP 数据核字第 20250GL246 号

策划编辑：闫 娉
责任编辑：樊川燕
封面设计：包荧莹
图文制作：史维肖
责任印制：吕 越
出 版 人：曾庆宇
出版发行：北京科学技术出版社
社 址：北京西直门南大街16号
邮政编码：100035
ISBN 978-7-5714-4473-0

电 话：0086-10-66135495（总编室）
0086-10-66113227（发行部）
网 址：www.bkydw.cn
印 刷：雅迪云印（天津）科技有限公司
开 本：889 mm × 1194 mm 1/16
字 数：165千字
印 张：8.25
版 次：2025年3月第1版
印 次：2025年3月第1次印刷

定 价：91.50元

Table of Contents

Introduction

“牛津技能世界：英语听说专项训练”系列将英语听力和英语口语的学习以灵活有趣的方式结合到一起，着眼于策略和技巧的教授，有助于学生自主学习并达成学习目标。

快来开启你的探险之旅吧！

大家好，我们是奥利和莫莉，也是牛津技能世界探险之旅的向导。我们会讲授实用的听力和口语学习策略，提出有针对性的问题并给出合理的建议，帮助你达成学习目标。相信在我们的陪伴下，你的探险之旅将充满乐趣！还在等什么？快开始吧！

Quick Guide

引入话题

话题贴近学生生活，且都基于特定的主题。

这里列出了每个单元*的学习目标。

奇闻趣事
旨在快速激发学生的学习兴趣。

奥利和莫莉会引导学生进行思考、合作与交流。

设置问题，激活学生的背景知识，引导学生进行思辨。

听前准备和听力训练

学生学习重点词汇，并在本书后面的“图解词典”中写出相应的单词或短语。

这里介绍了超级实用的听力学习策略。

听力学习策略能帮助学生应对不同类型的听力材料，不管是虚构类的还是非虚构类的。听录音的时候，学生应联系生活进行思辨。

* 每个话题包含两个主题相近的单元。

加深理解

引导学生运用听力学习策略来更好地理解听到的内容。

设置相关练习，帮助学生进一步掌握所学词汇。

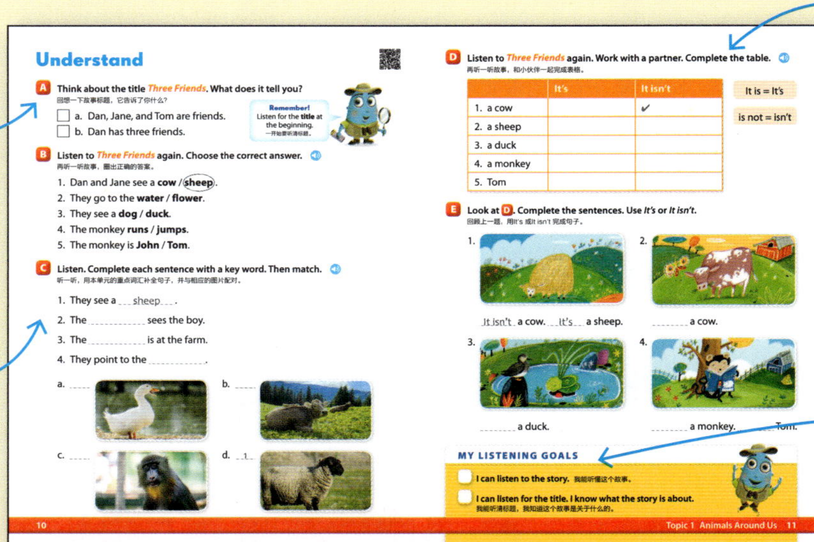
Understand

A Think about the title *Three Friends*. What does it tell you?
回想一下故事标题，它告诉了你什么？
a. Dan, Jane, and Tom are friends.
b. Dan has three friends.

Remember! Listen for the **title** at the beginning.

B Listen to *Three Friends* again. Choose the correct answer.
再听一听故事，圈出正确的答案。
1. Dan and Jane see a **cow / sheep**.
2. They go to the **water / flower**.
3. They see a **dog / duck**.
4. The monkey **runs / jumps**.
5. The monkey is **John / Tom**.

C Listen. Complete each sentence with a key word. Then match.
1. They see a ___sheep___.
2. The ________ sees the boy.
3. The ________ is at the farm.
4. They point to the ________.
a. ___ b. ___ c. ___ d. _1_

D Listen to *Three Friends* again. Work with a partner. Complete the table.
再听一听故事，和小伙伴一起完成表格。

	It's	It isn't
1. a cow		✓
2. a sheep		
3. a duck		
4. a monkey		
5. Tom		

It is = It's
is not = isn't

E Look at D. Complete the sentences. Use *It's* or *It isn't*.
1. _It isn't_ a cow. _It's_ a sheep.
2. ________ a cow.
3. ________ a duck.
4. ________ a monkey. ________ Tom.

MY LISTENING GOALS
I can listen to the story. 我能听懂这个故事。
I can listen for the title. I know what the story is about. 我能听清标题，我知道这个故事是关于什么的。

10 Topic 1 Animals Around Us 11

检验学生对本单元内容，包括词汇和语法的掌握程度。

设置更多练习，帮助学生了解不同的题型，以更好地应对考试。

听力测试

奥利和莫莉会引导学生运用学到的听力学习策略。

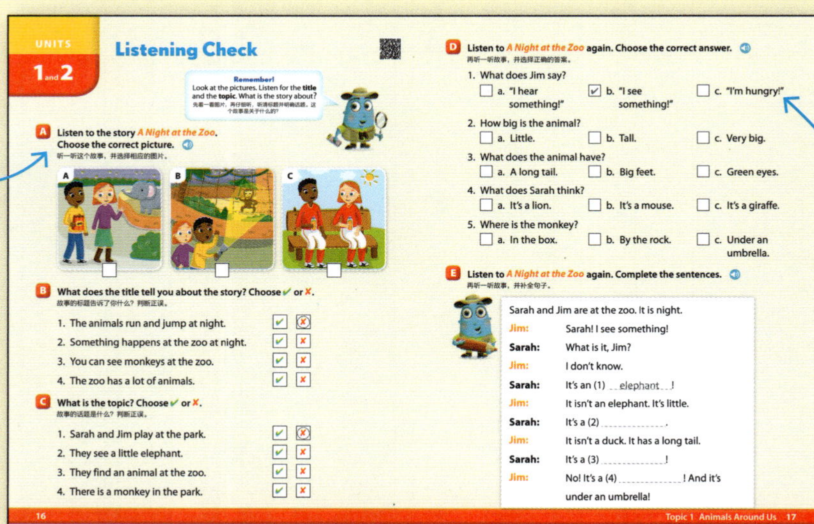
UNITS 1 and 2
Listening Check

Remember! Look at the pictures. Listen for the **title** and the **topic**. What is the story about?

A Listen to the story *A Night at the Zoo*. Choose the correct picture.
听一听这个故事，并选择相应的图片。
A B C

B What does the title tell you about the story? Choose ✓ or ✗.
故事的标题告诉了你什么？判断正误。
1. The animals run and jump at night.
2. Something happens at the zoo at night.
3. You can see monkeys at the zoo.
4. The zoo has a lot of animals.

C What is the topic? Choose ✓ or ✗.
故事的话题是什么？判断正误。
1. Sarah and Jim play at the park.
2. They see a little elephant.
3. They find an animal at the zoo.
4. There is a monkey in the park.

D Listen to *A Night at the Zoo* again. Choose the correct answer.
再听一听故事，并选择正确的答案。
1. What does Jim say? a. "I hear something!" b. "I see something!" c. "I'm hungry!"
2. How big is the animal? a. Little. b. Tall. c. Very big.
3. What does the animal have? a. A long tail. b. Big feet. c. Green eyes.
4. What does Sarah think? a. It's a lion. b. It's a mouse. c. It's a giraffe.
5. Where is the monkey? a. In the box. b. By the rock. c. Under an umbrella.

E Listen to *A Night at the Zoo* again. Complete the sentences.
再听一听故事，并补全句子。
Sarah and Jim are at the zoo. It is night.
Jim: Sarah! I see something!
Sarah: What is it, Jim?
Jim: I don't know.
Sarah: It's an (1) _elephant_!
Jim: It isn't an elephant. It's little.
Sarah: It's a (2) ________.
Jim: It isn't a duck. It has a long tail.
Sarah: It's a (3) ________!
Jim: No! It's a (4) ________! And it's under an umbrella!

16 Topic 1 Animals Around Us 17

学生完成相关练习，进一步强化听力理解和词汇运用能力。

口语交际和说一说

口语训练目标
旨在帮助学生在不同的场景下自信表达。

口语练习小贴士
提供语法、标点符号和学习策略方面的指导，帮助学生准确、流利地交流。

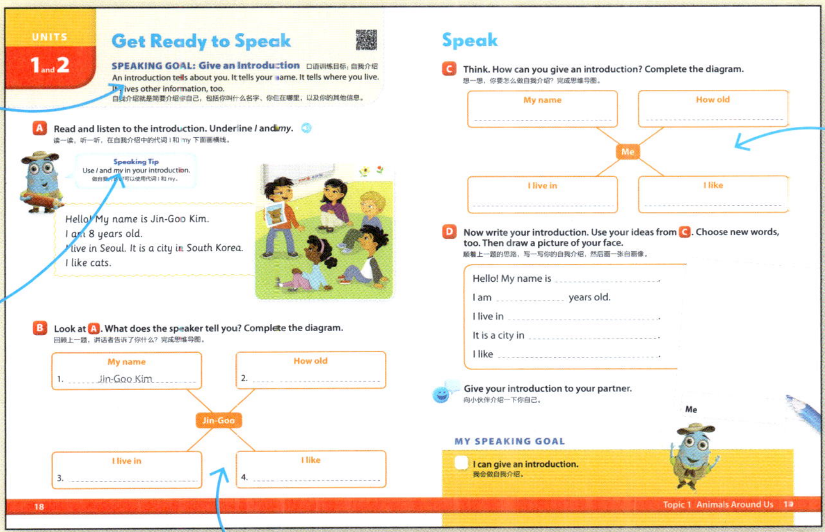
UNITS 1 and 2

Get Ready to Speak

SPEAKING GOAL: Give an Introduction

An introduction tells about you. It tells your name. It tells where you live. It gives other information, too.

A Read and listen to the introduction. Underline I and my.

Speaking Tip: Use I and my in your introduction.

Hello! My name is Jin-Goo Kim.
I am 8 years old.
I live in Seoul. It is a city in South Korea.
I like cats.

B Look at A. What does the speaker tell you? Complete the diagram.

My name: 1. Jin-Goo Kim | How old: 2. | I live in: 3. | I like: 4.

Speak

C Think. How can you give an introduction? Complete the diagram.

My name | How old | Me | I live in | I like

D Now write your introduction. Use your ideas from C. Choose new words, too. Then draw a picture of your face.

Hello! My name is ______.
I am ______ years old.
I live in ______.
It is a city in ______.
I like ______.

Give your introduction to your partner.

MY SPEAKING GOAL

I can give an introduction.

18 | Topic 1 Animals Around Us 19

提供“脚手架式”口语交际模板，帮助学生达成口语训练目标。

以思维导图的形式展示口语交际模板，帮助学生梳理思路。

练习册

设置形式多样的练习，帮助学生进一步运用所学的听力学习策略，提高听力理解能力。

WORKBOOK UNIT 2

Listen

LISTENING GOAL: Listen for the Topic

Remember! The topic is what the listening is about. Look at the title and pictures. They can tell you the topic.

A Listen to the conversation City Zoo. Then put the pictures in order.

B Think about City Zoo. What is the topic? Choose ✓ or ✗.

1. Don has an apple.
2. Amy and Don have fun at the zoo.
3. The zoo is too big.

C Listen to City Zoo again. Choose Yes or No.

1. Amy is hot. Yes No
2. There are seven crocodiles. Yes No
3. The elephant is under the tree. Yes No
4. Don and Amy see a giraffe. Yes No
5. Don is hungry. Yes No
6. There is a bee on the apple. Yes No

Workbook 93

设置丰富的词汇练习，帮助学生提高听力理解和词汇运用能力。

引导学生在交流中使用规范、通顺的语言。

D Listen. Then read and choose the correct answer.

1. What does the girl see? a. b. c.
2. What is at the zoo? a. b. c.
3. What is old? a. b. c.

E Complete the sentences.

1. The elephant is big.
2. The m______ is little.
3. The g______ is tall.
4. The c______ is very long.

Speak

Circle I and my.

I am 7 years old.
Jean is my friend.
I like my new game.

Remember! Use I and my to give an introduction.

94

TOPIC 1

SCIENCE

Animals Around Us

MY GOALS

UNIT 1

- Listen to the story *Three Friends*
- Listen for the title

UNIT 2

- Listen to the passage *Animal Fun*
- Listen for the topic

SPEAK

- Give an introduction

A **Look at the picture. What do you see?**
看图片，回答问题。

1. What animals do you see?
2. Do you like the animals? Why or why not?

FUN FACT

Listen

A Friendly Animal

B **Listen to the Fun Fact. Then answer the questions.** 听“奇闻趣事”，回答问题。

1. What does this animal do?
2. What is your favorite animal? Why do you like it?

Think, Pair, Share
What animals can you see at the zoo?
你能在动物园里看到什么动物？

UNIT 1

Get Ready to Listen

A Listen, point, and say. Write the words in your picture dictionary.

听一听，指一指，说一说。在"图解词典"中写出对应的单词。

cow

duck

monkey

sheep

B Listen and color. 听一听，涂一涂。

C Listen and write. 听一听，写一写。

1. sheep
2. ______
3. ______
4. ______

Listen

LISTENING GOAL: Listen for the Title 听力训练目标：听清标题

The title is the listening's name. It tells what the listening is about. Listen for the title at the beginning. 标题就是听力材料名，它能告诉我们听力材料是关于什么的。一开始要听清标题。

A **Listen. Then choose Yes or No.** 听一听，并判断正误。

1. *Mr. Frog* is about a frog. He likes rain. (Yes) No
2. *The Bananas* is about a boy. He wants some banana juice. Yes No
3. *Bird and the Books* is about a bird. He likes to read. Yes No

Three Friends

B **Listen to the story *Three Friends*. What is it about? Choose the correct picture.** 听一听这个故事讲了什么内容，并选择相应的图片。

A

☐

B

☐

Now put the sentences in order. 给句子排序。

a. Dan and Jane find Tom. ☐

b. Dan and Jane see two animals. 1

c. Dan and Jane go to a tree. ☐

Why is the **title** *Three Friends*?
为什么这个故事的标题是“Three Friends”？

Think!
What animals can you see on a farm?
你能在农场里看到什么动物?

Understand

A **Think about the title *Three Friends*. What does it tell you?**
回想一下故事标题，它告诉了你什么？

☐ a. Dan, Jane, and Tom are friends.
☐ b. Dan has three friends.

Remember!
Listen for the **title** at the beginning.
一开始要听清标题。

B **Listen to *Three Friends* again. Choose the correct answer.**
再听一听故事，圈出正确的答案。

1. Dan and Jane see a **cow** / **sheep**.
2. They go to the **water** / **flower**.
3. They see a **dog** / **duck**.
4. The monkey **runs** / **jumps**.
5. The monkey is **John** / **Tom**.

C **Listen. Complete each sentence with a key word. Then match.**
听一听，用本单元的重点词汇补全句子，并与相应的图片配对。

1. They see a __sheep__.
2. The ________ sees the boy.
3. The ________ is at the farm.
4. They point to the ________.

a. ____

b. ____

c. ____

d. __1__

D Listen to *Three Friends* again. Work with a partner. Complete the table.

再听一听故事，和小伙伴一起完成表格。

	It's	It isn't
1. a cow		✔
2. a sheep		
3. a duck		
4. a monkey		
5. Tom		

It is = It's

is not = isn't

E Look at D. Complete the sentences. Use *It's* or *It isn't*.

回顾上一题，用It's 或It isn't 完成句子。

1.

It isn't a cow. It's a sheep.

2.

______ a cow.

3.

______ a duck.

4.

______ a monkey. ______ Tom.

MY LISTENING GOALS

- ☐ **I can listen to the story.** 我能听懂这个故事。
- ☐ **I can listen for the title. I know what the story is about.**
  我能听清标题，我知道这个故事是关于什么的。

UNIT 2

Get Ready to Listen

A Listen, point, and say. Write the words in your picture dictionary.

听一听，指一指，说一说。在“图解词典”中写出对应的单词。

crocodile

elephant

giraffe

mouse

B Listen and number. 听一听，在圆圈里填上正确的序号。

C Listen and complete the sentences. 听一听，并补全句子。

1. The mouse eats a lot.
2. The ________ can run.
3. The ________ can kick.
4. The ________ likes bananas.

Listen

LISTENING GOAL: Listen for the Topic 听力训练目标：明确话题

The topic is what the listening is about. The title and pictures can tell you the topic.
话题告诉我们听力材料是关于什么的。标题和图片有助于你明确话题。

A Listen. Choose ✔ or ✘. 听一听，并判断正误。

1. 

✔ ✘

2. 

✔ ✘

3. 

✔ ✘

Animal Fun

B Listen to the passage *Animal Fun*. What is it about? Choose the correct picture.
听一听这篇文章讲了什么内容，并选择相应的图片。

A 

B 

Now choose ✔ or ✘. 判断正误。

1. The boys and girls see animals. ✔ ✘
2. The boys and girls are in a little car. ✔ ✘
3. The boys and girls are happy. ✔ ✘

Where can you find the **topic**?
你如何明确话题？

Think!

Do you want to go on a safari? Why or why not?
你想不想去游猎？为什么？

Understand

A Think about *Animal Fun*. What is the topic? Choose Yes or No.

回想一下这篇文章的话题是什么，并判断正误。

1. A safari. **Yes** **No**
2. Boys and girls on a bus. **Yes** **No**

Remember!
The **title** and **pictures** can tell you the topic.
标题和图片有助于你明确话题。

B Listen to *Animal Fun* again. Choose the correct answer.

再听一听文章，选择正确的答案。

1. Where is the crocodile?
   - ☐ a. On the grass. ☑ b. In the water.
2. Where is the giraffe?
   - ☐ a. By the water. ☐ b. Under the tree.
3. Where is the mouse?
   - ☐ a. By the bus. ☐ b. On the bus.

C Listen and choose the correct picture. Then write the key word.

听一听，选择恰当的图片，并将相应的词写在下方的横线上。

1.

☐ a

☑ b

giraffe

2.

☐ a

☐ b

____

3.

☐ a

☐ b

____

4.

☐ a

☐ b

____

D Listen to *Animal Fun* again. Complete the diagram.

再听一听文章，完成思维导图。

Where are the animals?

Crocodile	Elephant	Giraffe	Mouse
1. in the water	2. ________	3. ________	4. ________

E Look at D. Write. Use *in, on, under,* or *by*.

回顾上一题，用in、on、under或by完成句子。

1. 

The crocodile is ___in___ the water.

2. 

The elephant is ________ the grass.

3. 

The giraffe is ________ the tree.

4. 

The mouse is ________ the bus.

MY LISTENING GOALS

- ☐ I can listen to the passage. 我能听懂这篇文章。
- ☐ I can listen for the topic. I know what the listening is about. 我能明确话题，我知道这篇文章是关于什么的。

UNITS **1 and 2**

Listening Check

Remember!
Look at the pictures. Listen for the **title** and the **topic**. What is the story about?
先看一看图片，再仔细听，听清标题并明确话题。这个故事是关于什么的?

A Listen to the story *A Night at the Zoo*. Choose the correct picture.

听一听这个故事，并选择相应的图片。

B What does the title tell you about the story? Choose ✔ or ✘.

故事的标题告诉了你什么？判断正误。

1. The animals run and jump at night. ✔ ✘ (✘ circled)
2. Something happens at the zoo at night. ✔ ✘
3. You can see monkeys at the zoo. ✔ ✘
4. The zoo has a lot of animals. ✔ ✘

C What is the topic? Choose ✔ or ✘.

故事的话题是什么？判断正误。

1. Sarah and Jim play at the park. ✔ ✘ (✘ circled)
2. They see a little elephant. ✔ ✘
3. They find an animal at the zoo. ✔ ✘
4. There is a monkey in the park. ✔ ✘

D Listen to *A Night at the Zoo* again. Choose the correct answer.

再听一听故事，并选择正确的答案。

1. What does Jim say?
   - ☐ a. "I hear something!"
   - ☑ b. "I see something!"
   - ☐ c. "I'm hungry!"
2. How big is the animal?
   - ☐ a. Little.
   - ☐ b. Tall.
   - ☐ c. Very big.
3. What does the animal have?
   - ☐ a. A long tail.
   - ☐ b. Big feet.
   - ☐ c. Green eyes.
4. What does Sarah think?
   - ☐ a. It's a lion.
   - ☐ b. It's a mouse.
   - ☐ c. It's a giraffe.
5. Where is the monkey?
   - ☐ a. In the box.
   - ☐ b. By the rock.
   - ☐ c. Under an umbrella.

E Listen to *A Night at the Zoo* again. Complete the sentences.

再听一听故事，并补全句子。

Sarah and Jim are at the zoo. It is night.

Jim: Sarah! I see something!

Sarah: What is it, Jim?

Jim: I don't know.

Sarah: It's an (1) elephant !

Jim: It isn't an elephant. It's little.

Sarah: It's a (2) ________.

Jim: It isn't a duck. It has a long tail.

Sarah: It's a (3) ________!

Jim: No! It's a (4) ________! And it's under an umbrella!

UNITS 1 and 2

Get Ready to Speak

SPEAKING GOAL: Give an Introduction 口语训练目标：自我介绍

An introduction tells about you. It tells your name. It tells where you live. It gives other information, too.

自我介绍就是简要介绍你自己，包括你叫什么名字、你住在哪里，以及你的其他信息。

A Read and listen to the introduction. Underline *I* and *my*.

读一读，听一听，在自我介绍中的代词 I 和 my 下面画横线。

Speaking Tip

Use *I* and *my* in your introduction.

做自我介绍时可以使用代词 I 和 my。

Hello! My name is Jin-Goo Kim.

I am 8 years old.

I live in Seoul. It is a city in South Korea.

I like cats.

B Look at A. What does the speaker tell you? Complete the diagram.

回顾上一题，讲话者告诉了你什么？完成思维导图。

Jin-Goo

My name

1. Jin-Goo Kim

How old

2. ____________

I live in

3. ____________

I like

4. ____________

Speak

C **Think. How can you give an introduction? Complete the diagram.**

想一想，你要怎么做自我介绍？完成思维导图。

Me	
My name ________	How old ________
I live in ________	I like ________

D **Now write your introduction. Use your ideas from C. Choose new words, too. Then draw a picture of your face.**

顺着上一题的思路，写一写你的自我介绍，然后画一张自画像。

Hello! My name is ________.

I am ________ years old.

I live in ________.

It is a city in ________.

I like ________.

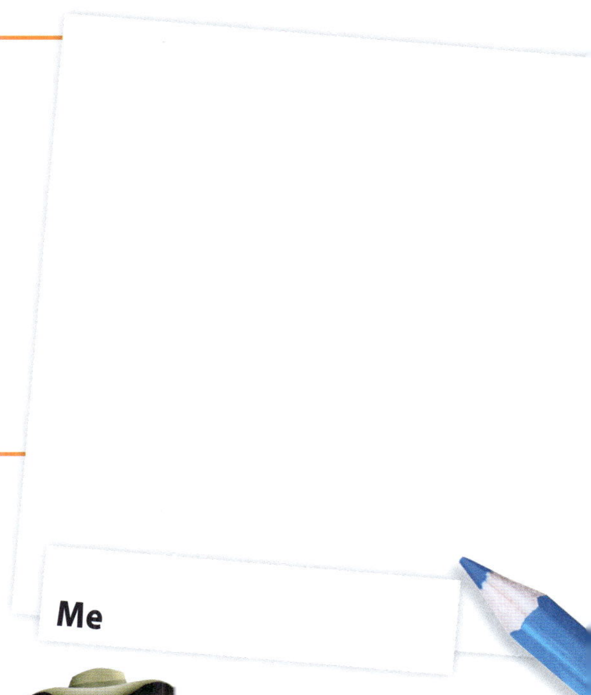

Give your introduction to your partner.

向小伙伴介绍一下你自己。

MY SPEAKING GOAL

☐ **I can give an introduction.**
我会做自我介绍。

TOPIC 2

ART

Red Circle, Blue Square

MY GOALS

UNIT 3

- Listen to the conversation *Cookie Count*
- Listen for numbers

UNIT 4

- Listen to the story *Fred the Clown*
- Listen for colors

SPEAK

- Give a description

A **Look at the picture. What do you see?**
看图片，回答问题。

1. How many people are there?
2. Where do you run?

FUN FACT

Listen

A Fun Run

B **Listen to the Fun Fact. Then answer the questions.** 听“奇闻趣事”，回答问题。

1. What do the people do?
2. Do you want to go on this run? Why or why not?

Think, Pair, Share
What colors do you like? Why? Where can you see the colors?
你喜欢什么颜色？为什么？你在哪里能看到这些颜色？

UNIT 3

Get Ready to Listen

A Listen, point, and say. Write the words in your picture dictionary.

听一听，指一指，说一说。在“图解词典”中写出对应的单词。

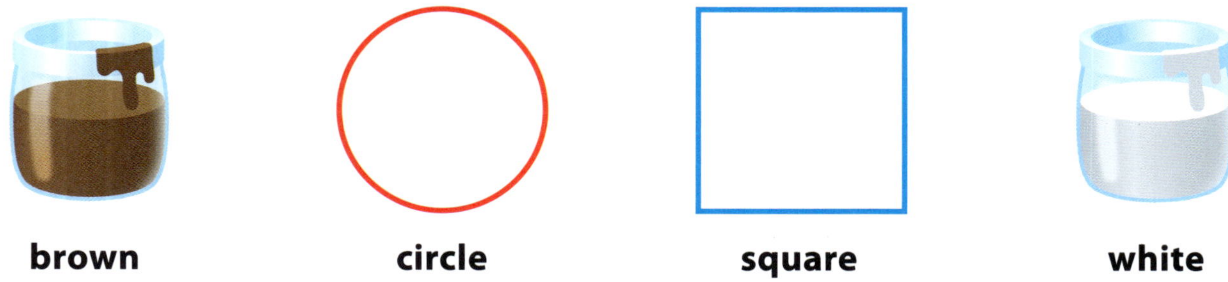

B Listen and color. 听一听，涂一涂。

C Listen and write. 听一听，写一写。

1. circle
2. ____________
3. ____________
4. ____________

Listen

LISTENING GOAL: Listen for Numbers 听力训练目标：听清数词

Words like *four* and *ten* are numbers. Numbers tell how many.

像 four 和 ten 这样的单词是英文中的数词。数词能告诉我们东西的数量。

A **Listen. Then complete the sentences.** 听一听，用数词补全句子。

1. She has __three__ dolls.
2. There is ________ train.
3. There are ________ pencils.

Cookie Count

B **Listen to the conversation *Cookie Count*. What is it about? Choose the correct picture.**

听一听这段对话讲了什么内容，并选择相应的图片。

A  ☐

B  ☐

Now put the sentences in order. 给句子排序。

a. Hannah sees Oscar. [1]

b. Oscar eats one cookie. [ ]

c. Oscar looks at the cookies. [ ]

What are the **numbers**?
对话中提到了哪些数词？

Think! What cookies do you like?
你喜欢什么样的饼干？

Understand

Remember!
Numbers help us understand how many.
数词能帮助我们了解具体数量。

A **Think about *Cookie Count*.**
How many cookies are there?
回想一下对话，里面提到了多少块饼干？

- ☐ a. Oscar eats one cookie. There are seven cookies left.
- ☐ b. Oscar eats one cookie. There are eight cookies left.

B **Listen to *Cookie Count* again. Choose the correct answer.**
再听一听对话，圈出正确的答案。

1. **Oscar** / **Hannah** has cookies.
2. There are **two** / **three** colors.
3. There are **white** / **purple** cookies.
4. There are **pink** / **brown** cookies.
5. There are **three** / **four** square cookies.

C **Listen. Complete each sentence with a key word. Then match.**
听一听，用本单元的重点词汇补全句子，并与相应的图片配对。

1. This is a __square__.
2. The teapot is ______.
3. It's a ______ nest.
4. It's a ______.

a. ____

b. __1__

c. ____

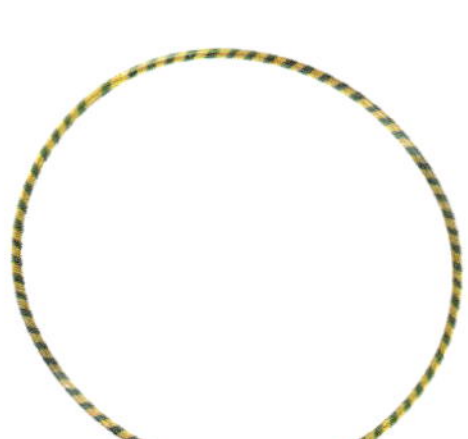

d. ____

D Listen to *Cookie Count* again. Complete the diagram.

再听一听对话，完成思维导图。

Cookie Count

1. Cookies	2. Cookies
Color: brown	Color: ______
Shape: ______	Shape: ______

E Look at D. Complete the sentences. Use *this*, *is*, *brown*, or *white*.

回顾上一题，用this、is、brown或white完成句子。

1.

Is this a circle?

Yes, it is. It's a circle.

2.

Is ______ a circle?

No, it isn't. It's a square.

3.

______ this a white circle?

No, it isn't. It's a ______ circle.

4.

Is ______ a brown square?

No, it isn't. It's a ______ square.

MY LISTENING GOALS

- [ ] I can listen to the conversation. 我能听懂这段对话。
- [ ] I can listen for numbers. Numbers tell how many. 我能听清对话中的数词。数词能告诉我们东西的数量。

UNIT 4

Get Ready to Listen

Let's learn the **key words**.
一起来学习重点词汇吧！

A **Listen, point, and say. Write the words in your picture dictionary.**
听一听，指一指，说一说。在“图解词典”中写出对应的单词。

blue

green

red

yellow

B **Listen and number.** 听一听，在圆圈里填上正确的序号。

C **Listen and complete the sentences.** 听一听，并补全句子。

1. The pencil is ___green___.
2. He has a ________ vest.
3. She is in the ________ car.
4. I have a ________ yo-yo.

Listen

LISTENING GOAL: Listen for Colors 听力训练目标：听清颜色词

Words like *red* and *blue* are colors. Listen for color words. They tell what color things are.
像 red 和 blue 这样的单词是英文中的颜色词。注意听颜色词，它们能告诉我们东西是什么颜色的。

A **Listen. Choose ✔ or ✘.** 听一听，并判断正误。

1. 

(✔) ✘

2. 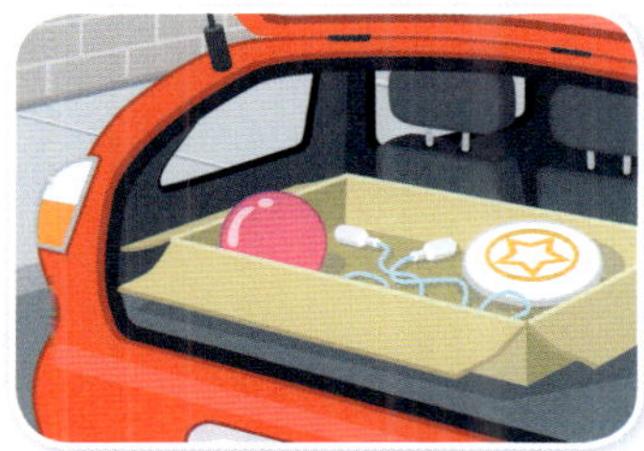

✔ ✘

3. 

✔ ✘

Fred the Clown

B **Listen to the story *Fred the Clown*. What is it about? Choose the correct picture.** 听一听这个故事讲了什么内容，并选择相应的图片。

A 

☐

B 

☐

Now choose ✔ or ✘. 判断正误。

1. Fred doesn't have the car. (✔) ✘
2. Fred sees Joe. ✔ ✘
3. Joe has Fred's guitar. ✔ ✘

What **color** is Fred's car?
弗雷德的汽车是什么颜色的？

Think!

What colors are your toys? What colors are your friends' toys?
你的玩具都是什么颜色的呢？你朋友们的玩具又是什么颜色的？

Understand

Remember!
Color words tell what color things are.
颜色词能告诉我们东西是什么颜色的。

A Think about *Fred the Clown*.
What color words are in the story? Choose Yes or No.

回想一下故事，里面提到了哪些颜色词？判断正误。

1. Black, orange, pink, purple. **Yes** **No**
2. Red, yellow, green, blue. **Yes** **No**

B Listen to *Fred the Clown* again. Choose the correct answer.

再听一听故事，选择正确的答案。

1. Who has Fred's car?
   ☑ a. Joe. ☐ b. Jim.
2. What color is Fred's skateboard?
   ☐ a. Orange. ☐ b. Red.
3. What color is Fred's balloon?
   ☐ a. Blue. ☐ b. Purple.

C Listen and choose the correct picture. Then write the key word.

听一听，选择恰当的图片，并将相应的词写在下方的横线上。

1.
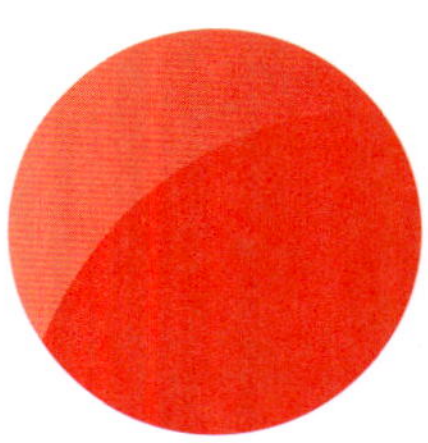

☐ a ☑ b
green

2.
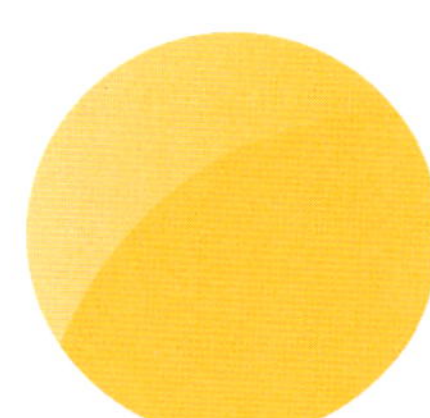

☐ a ☐ b
____

3.
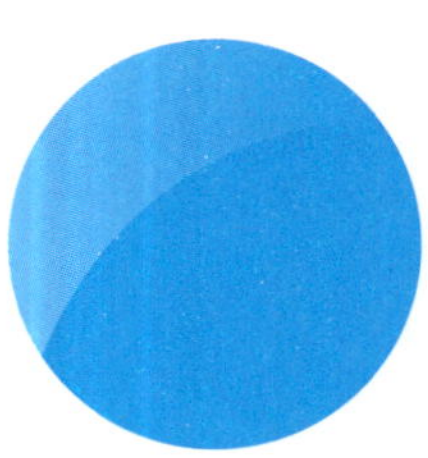

☐ a ☐ b
____

4.

☐ a ☐ b
____

D Listen to *Fred the Clown* again. Work with a partner. Complete the diagram.

再听一听故事，和小伙伴一起完成思维导图。

What does Fred have?

1. a green guitar
2. ________
3. ________
4. ________

E Look at D. Write. Use *have, has,* or *don't have.*

回顾上一题，用have、has或don't have完成句子。

1.

He ___has___ a green guitar.

2.

He ________ a red skateboard.

3.

I ________ an orange balloon.

I ________ a blue balloon.

4.

I ________ my car.

You ________ my yellow car!

MY LISTENING GOALS

- [ ] **I can listen to the story.** 我能听懂这个故事。
- [ ] **I can listen for color words. They tell what color things are.** 我能听清颜色词，这些词能告诉我们东西是什么颜色的。

UNITS 3 and 4

Listening Check

Remember!
Listen for **numbers**. They tell how many. Listen for **color words**. They tell what color things are.
注意听数词，数词能告诉我们东西的具体数量。还要注意听颜色词，这些词能告诉我们东西是什么颜色的。

A Listen to the poem *Traffic Light*. Choose the correct picture.
听一听这首诗，并选择相应的图片。

A

☐

B

☐

C

☐

B Read the sentences. Are the numbers correct? Choose ✔ or ✘.
读一读下面的句子，里面关于数量的表述正确吗？根据听到的内容判断正误。

1. There are two circles. ✔ ✘
2. There is one red circle. ✔ ✘
3. There is one black box. ✔ ✘
4. There are three squares. ✔ ✘

C Read the sentences. Are the colors correct? Choose ✔ or ✘.
读一读下面的句子，里面关于颜色的表述正确吗？根据听到的内容判断正误。

1. There is one green circle. ✔ ✘
2. Yellow says “slow.” ✔ ✘
3. There is one black circle. ✔ ✘
4. Green says “stop.” ✔ ✘

D Listen to *Traffic Light* again. Choose the correct answer.

再听一听这首诗，并选择正确的答案。

1. What shape is green?

   ☐ a. A square.　　☑ b. A circle.　　☐ c. A rectangle.

2. What does red say?

   ☐ a. Go.　　☐ b. Slow.　　☐ c. Stop.

3. How many yellow circles are there?

   ☐ a. One.　　☐ b. Two.　　☐ c. Three.

4. How many colors are there?

   ☐ a. Three.　　☐ b. Four.　　☐ c. Five.

5. What is / are in the poem?

   ☐ a. A pen.　　☐ b. Crayons.　　☐ c. A pencil.

E Listen to *Traffic Light* again. Complete the sentences.

再听一听这首诗，并补全句子。

I draw three (1) ____circles____.
One, two, three.
I see circles.
Red, (2) ________, green.
I have (3) ________.
Red says "stop!"
I have yellow.
Yellow says "slow."
I have green.
(4) ________ says "go!"
One black box. I have black.
This is a traffic light.
Go, crayons, go!
Vrooom!

UNITS 3 and 4

Get Ready to Speak

SPEAKING GOAL: Give a Description 口语训练目标：描述

A description tells what something looks like. It can be about people, places, or things.

描述就是告诉别人某人、某地或者某物是什么样子的。

A Read and listen to the description. What words tell about the tree? What words tell about the sun? Circle the words.

读一读，听一听。哪些单词是描述树的？哪些单词是描述太阳的？把这些单词圈出来。

Speaking Tip
Use color and shape words in your description.
在描述时使用表示颜色和形状的单词。

The Park

This is a tree. It's big.
It's green and brown.
This is the sun. It's a circle.
It's yellow.

B Look at **A**. What does the speaker say? Use the words from the description. Complete the diagram.

回顾上一题，讲话者说了什么？根据圈出的单词完成思维导图。

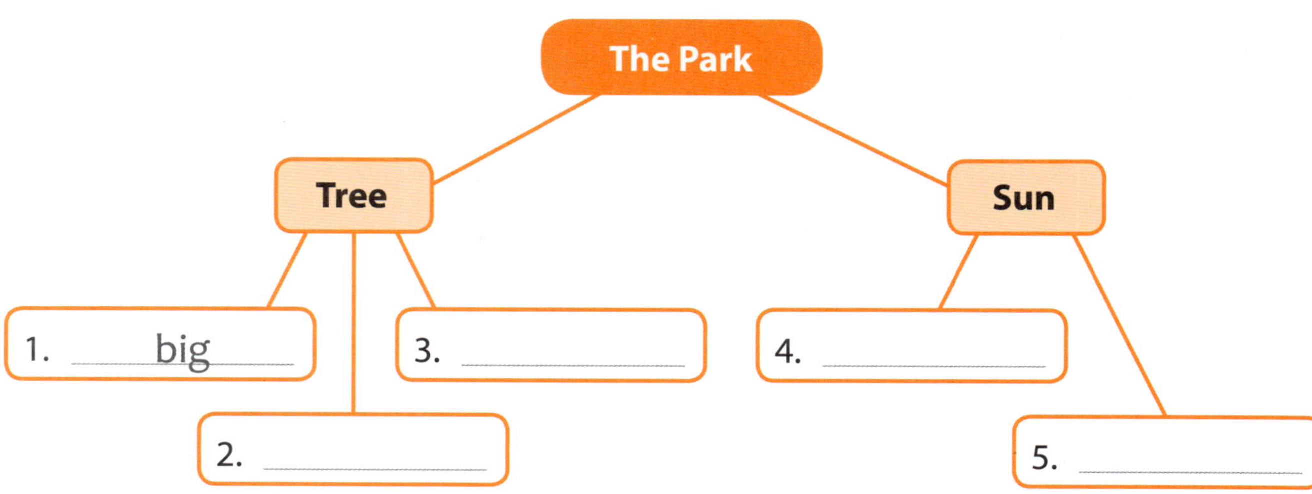

Speak

C **Think about a favorite place. What words tell about the place? Complete the diagram.** 想一处你最喜欢的地方。哪些单词可以描述这个地方？完成思维导图。

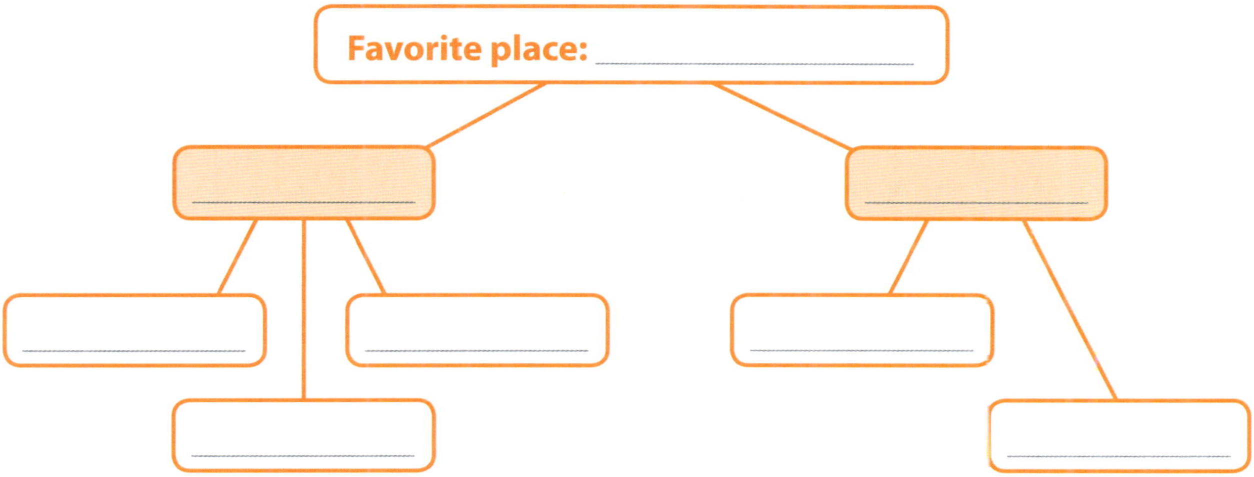

D **Now write your description. Use your ideas from C. Choose new words, too. Then draw a picture of the place.**
顺着上一题的思路，描述一下你最喜欢的地方，然后把它画出来。

This is ____________.
It's ____________.
It's ____________ and ____________.
This is ____________.
It's ____________.
It's ____________.

Give your description to your partner. Use your picture.
结合你的画给小伙伴描述一下这个地方。

MY SPEAKING GOAL

☐ **I can give a description.**
我会描述。

TOPIC

3

SOCIAL STUDIES

School Days

MY GOALS

UNIT 5

- Listen to the story *The Special Notebook*
- Listen for greetings and endings

UNIT 6

- Listen to the conversation *The Box*
- Listen for key words

SPEAK

- Use greetings and endings

A **Look at the picture. What do you see?**
看图片，回答问题。

1. Where are the children?
2. Do you like robots? Why or why not?

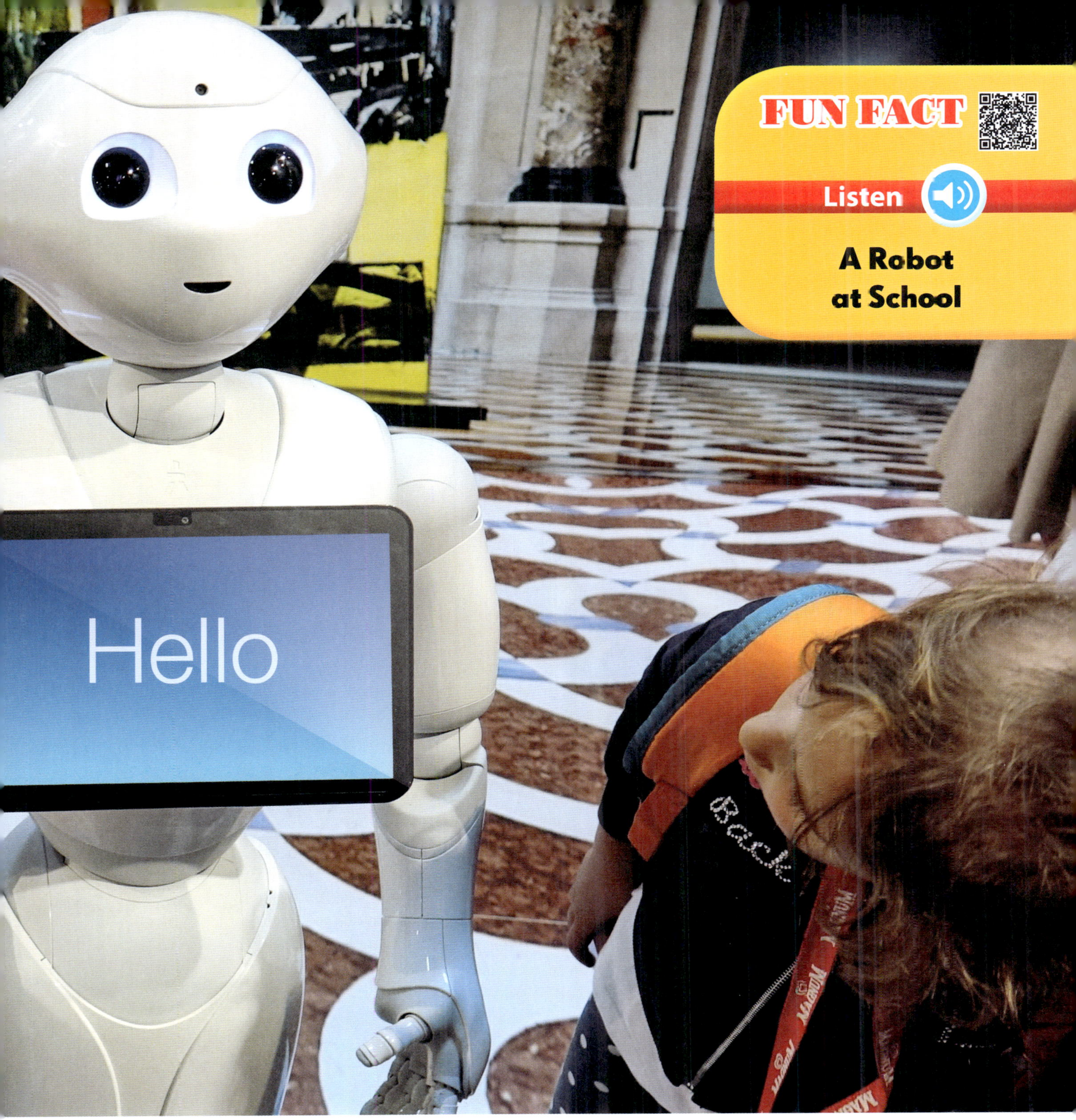

FUN FACT

Listen

A Robot at School

B **Listen to the Fun Fact. Then answer the questions.** 听“奇闻趣事”，回答问题。

1. What can the robot do?
2. Can a robot help you at school? What can it do?

Think, Pair, Share
What things do you have at your school?
你们学校有什么高科技的东西？

UNIT 5

Get Ready to Listen

Let's learn the **key words**.
一起来学习重点词汇吧!

A Listen, point, and say. Write the words in your picture dictionary.

听一听，指一指，说一说。在“图解词典”中写出对应的单词。

draw

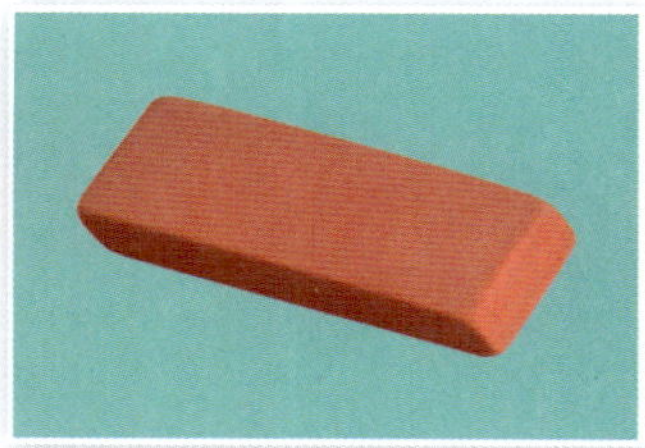

eraser

notebook

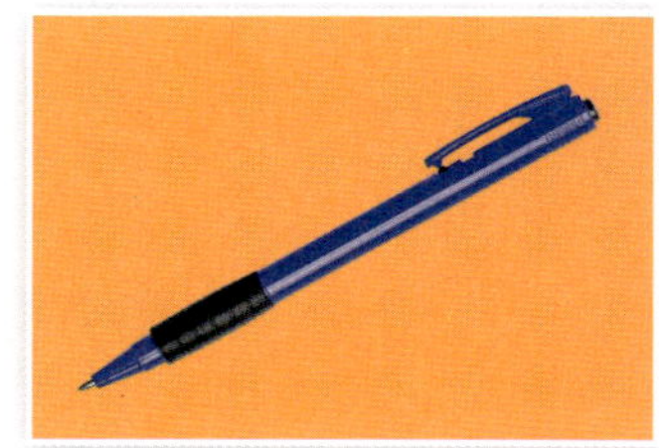

pen

B Listen and color. 听一听，涂一涂。

C Listen and write. 听一听，写一写。

1. notebook
2. ______
3. ______
4. ______

Listen

LISTENING GOAL: Listen for Greetings and Endings 听力训练目标：听清问候语和结束语

Greetings start a conversation. They are words like *hello* or *hi*. Endings stop a conversation. They are words like *goodbye* or *see you later*. 像hello和hi这样的单词是英语中的问候语，用于展开对话。像goodbye和see you later这样的单词和短语是英语中的结束语，用于结束对话。

A **Listen. Then complete the sentences.** 听一听，并补全句子。

1. The greeting is ____hi____.
2. The ending is ____________.
3. The teacher says ____________ to Kayo.

The Special Notebook

B **Listen to the story *The Special Notebook*. What is it about? Choose the correct picture.**
听一听这个故事讲了什么内容，并选择相应的图片。

A

☐

B

☐

Now put the sentences in order. 给句子排序。

a. Mei and Paul go to the zoo. ☐

b. Paul uses the eraser. ☐

c. Paul draws a picture. 1

What does Paul say at the **end**?
保罗最后说了什么？

Think!
Where do you want to go?
你想去哪里？

Understand

A Think about *The Special Notebook*. What is the greeting? What are the endings? Choose the correct answer.

回想一下故事，里面有哪些问候语和结束语？选择正确的答案。

☐ a. *Hello*, *we're home*, and *goodbye*.

☐ b. *Hi*, *see you later*, and *goodbye*.

Remember!
Greetings start a conversation. **Endings** stop a conversation.
问候语用于展开对话，结束语用于结束对话。

B Listen to *The Special Notebook* again. Choose the correct answer.

再听一听故事，圈出正确的答案。

1. Paul has a **crayon** / **notebook**.
2. He draws a **beach** / **zoo**.
3. Paul and Mei see a **lion** / **crocodile**.
4. Paul has **a book bag** / **an eraser**.
5. Mei **likes** / **doesn't like** the notebook.

C Listen. Complete each sentence with a key word. Then match.

听一听，用本单元的重点词汇补全句子，并与相应的图片配对。

1. This is my ___pen___.
2. The ________ is little.
3. I ________ at the table.
4. It's my ________.

a. ____

b. __1__

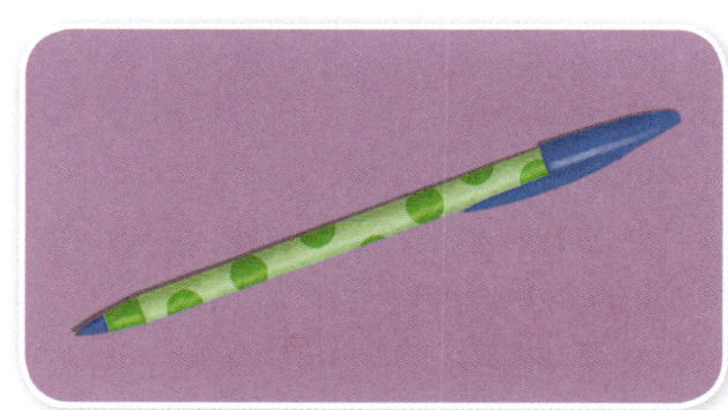

c. ____

d. ____

D Listen to *The Special Notebook* again. Work with a partner. Complete the diagram. 再听一听故事，和小伙伴一起完成思维导图。

What does Paul have?

1. ____notebook____
2. ______________
3. ______________
4. ______________

E Look at D. Complete the sentences. Use *is*, *this*, or *my*.

回顾上一题，用is、this或my完成句子。

1.

This ____is____ my notebook.

2.

This is ____________ pen.

3.

This ____________ my pencil.

4.

____________ is my eraser.

MY LISTENING GOALS

- [ ] I can listen to the story. 我能听懂这个故事。
- [ ] I can listen for greetings and endings. They start and stop a conversation.
我能听清故事中的问候语和结束语。问候语用于展开对话，结束语用于结束对话。

UNIT

6

Get Ready to Listen

Let's learn the **key words**.
一起来学习重点词汇吧！

A Listen, point, and say. Write the words in your picture dictionary.

听一听，指一指，说一说。在“图解词典”中写出对应的单词。

backpack

class

paper

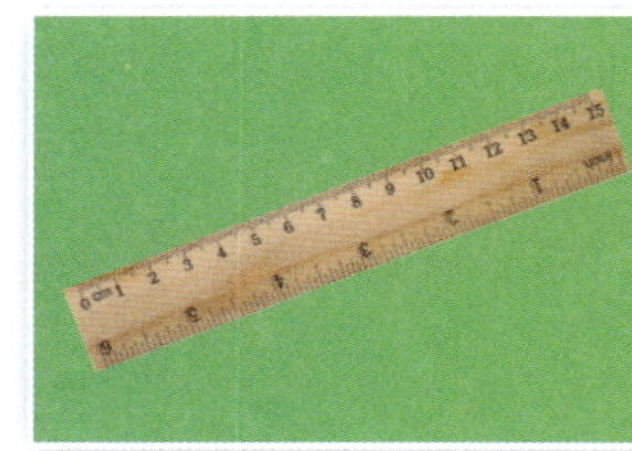

ruler

B Listen and number. 听一听，在圆圈里填上正确的序号。

C Listen and complete the sentences. 听一听，并补全句子。

1. The ___paper___ is in the cupboard.
2. This is my ________.
3. It's a ________.
4. I have a big ________.

Listen

LISTENING GOAL: Listen for Key Words 听力训练目标：抓住关键词

Key words are words you hear many times. Key words tell what the listening is about.
录音中频繁出现的单词就是关键词。关键词能告诉我们听力材料是关于什么的。

A Listen. Choose the correct answer. 听一听，并圈出正确的答案。

1. The key word is **pencil** / **long**.
2. The key word is **notebook** / **book**.
3. The key word is **table** / **flower**.

The Box

B Listen to the conversation *The Box*. What is it about? Choose the correct picture.
听一听这段对话讲了什么内容，并选择相应的图片。

A

☐

B

☐

Now choose ✔ or ✘. 判断正误。

1. There are two people. ✔ ✘
2. The boy talks to his aunt. ✔ ✘
3. The boy talks with his mom. ✔ ✘

What words do they say **many times**?
哪些词被反复提到？

Think!
What present do you want? Why?
你想要什么礼物？为什么？

Understand

Remember!
You hear **key words** many times.
关键词会出现很多次。

A **Think about *The Box*. What are the key words? Choose Yes or No.** 回想一下对话，对话的关键词是什么？判断正误。

1. *Box* and *class*. **Yes** **No**
2. *Present* and *backpack*. **Yes** **No**

B **Listen to *The Box* again. Choose the correct answer.**
再听一听对话，选择正确的答案。

1. Who gives a present to the boy?
   - ☐ a. His teacher.
   - ☑ b. His mom.
2. What is in the box?
   - ☐ a. A backpack.
   - ☐ b. A ruler.
3. Where can he take the present?
   - ☐ a. To class.
   - ☐ b. To the store.

C **Listen and choose the correct picture. Then write the key word.**
听一听，选择恰当的图片，并将相应的词写在下方的横线上。

1.

☐ a

☑ b

backpack

2.
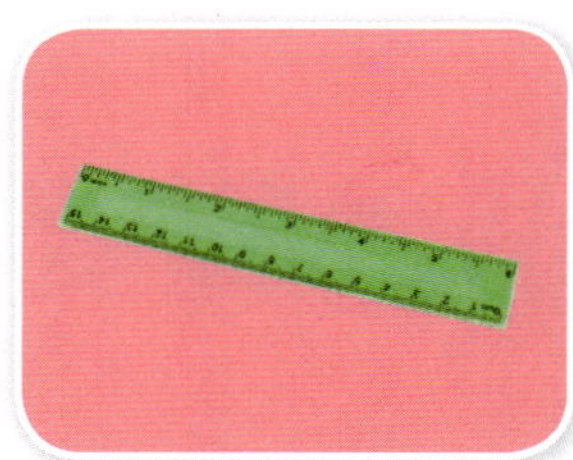
☐ a

☐ b

______

3.

☐ a

☐ b

______

4.
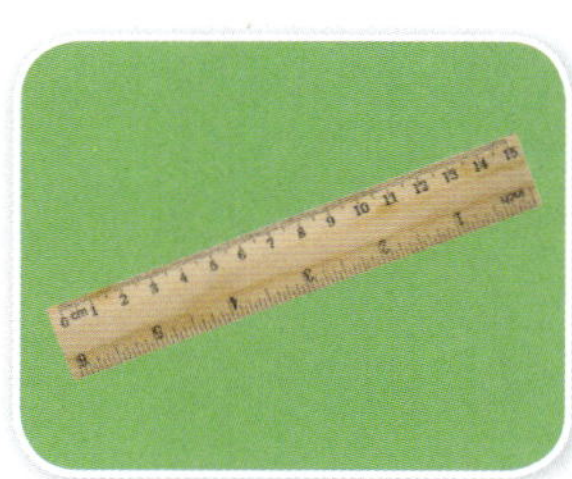
☐ a

☐ b

______

D Listen to *The Box* again. What are some questions? Work with a partner. Complete the diagram.

再听一听对话，里面都提了哪些问题？和小伙伴一起完成思维导图。

Questions

1. ___What's___ in the box?
2. ________ a ruler?
3. ________ paper?
4. ________ a backpack?

E Look at D. Write. Use *is, it,* or *isn't.* 回顾上一题，用is、it或isn't完成句子。

1\.

What's in the box?

___It___'s a present.

2\.

________ it a ruler?

No, it isn't.

3\.

Is it paper?

No, it ________.

4\.

Is ________ a backpack?

Yes, ________ is!

MY LISTENING GOALS

- ☐ I can listen to the conversation. 我能听懂这段对话。
- ☐ I can listen for key words. They tell what the listening is about. 我能抓住关键词，关键词能告诉我们听力材料是关于什么的。

UNITS 5 and 6

Listening Check

Remember!
Listen for **greetings** and **endings**. When do you hear them? Listen for **key words**. What is the listening about?
注意听问候语和结束语，它们是什么时候出现的？还要注意听关键词。这段听力材料是关于什么的？

A Listen to the story *Mouse and Frog*. Choose the correct picture.

听一听这个故事，并选择相应的图片。

B What is the greeting in the story? What is the ending? Choose ✔ or ✘.

这个故事里的问候语是什么？结束语又是什么？根据听到的内容判断正误。

1. Hi. ✔ ✘
2. Hello. ✔ ✘
3. Goodbye. ✔ ✘
4. See you later. ✔ ✘

C What are the key words? Choose ✔ or ✘.

这个故事的关键词是什么？根据听到的内容判断正误。

1. Pen. ✔ ✘
2. Backpack. ✔ ✘
3. Paper. ✔ ✘
4. Eraser. ✔ ✘

D Listen to *Mouse and Frog* again. Choose the correct answer.

再听一听故事，并选择正确的答案。

1. Who has a backpack?
   - ☐ a. Frog.
   - ☑ b. Mouse.
   - ☐ c. Bird.
2. What does Mouse have?
   - ☐ a. A ruler.
   - ☐ b. A pencil.
   - ☐ c. A pen.
3. Where is the paper?
   - ☐ a. In the desk.
   - ☐ b. At home.
   - ☐ c. In the backpack.
4. What does Mouse do?
   - ☐ a. He jumps.
   - ☐ b. He dances.
   - ☐ c. He eats.
5. Who finds the eraser?
   - ☐ a. Frog.
   - ☐ b. Mouse.
   - ☐ c. The teacher.

E Listen to *Mouse and Frog* again. Complete the sentences.

再听一听故事，并补全句子。

"Hello, Mouse!" says Frog.

"Hello, Frog! Look in my (1) backpack !

I have a pen and (2) ________.

And this is my eraser."

Mouse is happy. He jumps.

The (3) ________ and eraser jump, too.

"Where are my pen and eraser?"

"This is your pen.

This is your (4) ________!" says Frog.

"Thank you!"

"See you later!" says Frog.

UNITS 5 and 6

Get Ready to Speak

SPEAKING GOAL: Use Greetings and Endings

口语训练目标：在对话中使用问候语和结束语

A conversation is a talk between two or more people. Conversations have greetings and endings.

对话是指两人或多人间的交谈。对话中应包含问候语和结束语。

A Read and listen to the conversation. Underline the greetings. Underline the endings.

读一读，听一听，在问候语和结束语下面画横线。

Speaking Tip

Use words like *hello* or *hi* to start a conversation. Use words like *goodbye* or *see you later* to end it.

用hello和hi之类的问候语展开对话，用goodbye和see you later之类的结束语结束对话。

Trang: Hello, Mark!

Mark: Hi, Trang!

Trang: Look! I have a doll in my backpack!

Mark: It's a nice doll!

Trang: Thank you. See you later!

Mark: Goodbye, Trang!

B Look at **A**. What are the greetings? What are the endings? Complete the diagram.

回顾上一题，哪些是问候语？哪些是结束语？完成思维导图。

Greetings and Endings

1. hello
2. ________
3. ________
4. ________

Speak

C Think about your conversations. What greetings do you use? What endings do you use? Complete the diagram.

想一想，你在对话中会用到哪些问候语和结束语？完成思维导图。

Greetings and Endings

D Now work with your partner. Write a conversation about a backpack. What's in it? Use your greetings and endings from **C**.
Then draw the things in the backpack.

和小伙伴一起，顺着上一题的思路，围绕背包写一段对话。对话中要用到问候语和结束语。背包里都有哪些东西呢？把它们画出来。

Me: ____________, ____________.

My partner: ____________, ____________!

Me: Look! I have a(n) ____________ in my backpack!

My partner: It's a nice ____________!

Me: ____________. ____________!

My partner: ____________, ____________!

Say your conversation with your partner.

和小伙伴一起演练你们写的对话。

MY SPEAKING GOAL

☐ I can use greetings. I can use endings.

我会使用问候语和结束语。

TOPIC 4

Me and My Family

SOCIAL STUDIES

MY GOALS

UNIT 7

- Listen to the story *My Family*
- Listen for questions

UNIT 8

- Listen to the presentation *My Summer*
- Listen for answers

SPEAK

- Ask questions to find information

A **Look at the picture. What do you see?**
看图片，回答问题。

1. What's funny about this picture?
2. Do you like watermelon? What's your favorite fruit?

FUN FACT

Listen

Watermelon Fun

B **Listen to the Fun Fact. Then answer the questions.** 听“奇闻趣事”，回答问题。

1. Do they eat fast or slow? Do they eat a little or a lot?
2. What games do you like?

Think, Pair, Share
What games do you play with your family?
你会和家人一起做什么游戏？

UNIT 7

Get Ready to Listen

Let's learn the **key words**.
一起来学习重点词汇吧！

A Listen, point, and say. Write the words in your picture dictionary.

听一听，指一指，说一说。在“图解词典”中写出对应的单词。

parents

boy

girl

children

B Listen and color. 听一听，涂一涂。

C Listen and write. 听一听，写一写。

1. girl
2. ______
3. ______
4. ______

Listen

LISTENING GOAL: Listen for Questions 听力训练目标：听清问题

Questions ask for information. They begin with words like *what*, *where*, or *who*. Listen for these words. 问题旨在询问具体信息，英文问句通常由what、where或者who等疑问词引导。注意听带有这些疑问词的句子。

A **Listen. Then complete the sentences.** 听一听，并补全句子。

1. The question word is who.
2. The question word is ______.
3. The question word is ______.

My Family

B **Listen to the story *My Family*. What is it about? Choose the correct picture.** 听一听这个故事讲了什么内容，并选择相应的图片。

A

B

Now choose ✔ or ✘. 判断正误。

1. Meg looks at a picture. ✔ ✘ (✔ circled)
2. The picture shows Rosa's family. ✔ ✘
3. The family has four children. ✔ ✘

What are the **question words**?
故事中有哪些疑问词？

Think!
Where do you go with your family?
你会和家人去哪里？

Understand

A **Think about *My Family*. What question is in the story?**

回想一下故事，里面提了什么问题?

☐ a. Where is the boy?

☐ b. Who are they?

Remember!
Questions ask for information.
问题旨在询问具体信息。

B **Listen to *My Family* again. Choose the correct answer.**

再听一听故事，圈出正确的答案。

1. The picture shows (**Matt's**) / **Meg's** parents.
2. They are at the **beach** / **playground**.
3. The boy's name is **Jason** / **Jack**.
4. Jessie is a **boy** / **girl**.
5. Matt **likes** / **doesn't like** fish.

C **Listen. Complete each sentence with a key word. Then match.**

听一听，用本单元的重点词汇补全句子，并与相应的图片配对。

1. My __parents__ are at the beach.
2. I can see the ________.
3. The ________ has a cup.
4. The ________ has a cup, too.

a. ____

b. __1__

c. ____

d. ____

D Listen to *My Family* again. What are the questions? Complete the diagram.

再听一听故事，里面提了哪些问题？完成思维导图。

Questions

1. ______Who______ are they?
2. ____________ is this?
3. ____________ are the children?
4. ____________ is this?

E Look at D. Write the questions. Use *who*, *where*, or *what*.

回顾上一题，用who、where或what写问句。

1. 

______Who are they?______

They are my parents.

2. 

____

This is the beach.

3. 

____

They are Jason and Jessie.

4. 

____

It's fish.

MY LISTENING GOALS

- ☐ **I can listen to the story.** 我能听懂这个故事。
- ☐ **I can listen for questions.** 我能听清故事中的问题。

UNIT

8

Get Ready to Listen

A Listen, point, and say. Write the words in your picture dictionary.

听一听，指一指，说一说。在“图解词典”中写出对应的单词。

grandparents

uncle

cousin

family

B Listen and number. 听一听，在圆圈里填上正确的序号。

C Listen and complete the sentences. 听一听，并补全句子。

1. My ___grandparents___ are at home.
2. The teacher talks to my ______________.
3. My ______________ likes pizza.
4. My ______________ is in my class.

Listen

LISTENING GOAL: Listen for Answers 听力训练目标：听清答案

We say answers after questions. Answers give information. Listen to the questions. Then listen to what comes next.

提问后我们一般会给出答案，答案能传达信息。注意听问题和问题后面的答案。

A Listen. Does the picture show the answer? Choose ✓ or ✗.

听一听，图片是否准确描述了答案？判断正误。

1. 

☑ ✓ ☐ ✗

2. 

☐ ✓ ☐ ✗

3. 

☐ ✓ ☐ ✗

B Listen to the presentation *My Summer*. What is it about? Choose the correct picture.

听一听讲话者在课堂上展示了什么内容，并选择相应的图片。

My Summer

A

☐

B

☐

Now put the sentences in order. 给句子排序。

a. The family goes to the grandparents' house. [1]

b. The boy and his uncle ride bicycles. [ ]

c. They play a game. [ ]

What do we get from **answers**?
答案告诉了我们什么？

Think!

What do you do in the summer?
夏天时，你通常会做什么？

Understand

A **Think about *My Summer*. What answer is in the presentation? Choose Yes or No.**
回想一下课堂展示的内容，里面出现过的答案是哪个？判断正误。

1. He's my uncle. **Yes** **No**
2. These are my parents. **Yes** **No**

Remember!
Listen for an **answer** after a question.
注意听问题后面的答案。

B **Listen to *My Summer* again. Choose the correct answer.**
再听一听这场课堂展示，选择正确的答案。

1. What is in the picture?
   - ☑ a. The grandparents' house.
   - ☐ b. The parents' house.
2. What does the boy do?
   - ☐ a. He plays a game.
   - ☐ b. He swims.
3. Who is tall?
   - ☐ a. The cousin.
   - ☐ b. The uncle.

C **Listen and choose the correct picture. Then write the key word.**
听一听，选择恰当的图片，并将相应的词写在下方的横线上。

1.

☐ a

☑ b

grandparents

2.

☐ a

☐ b

3.

☐ a

☐ b

4.

☐ a

☐ b

D **Listen to *My Summer* again. What word tells about each person or thing? Work with a partner. Complete the diagram.**

再听一听这场课堂展示，里面分别用哪些词描述了提到的人或物？和小伙伴一起完成思维导图。

My Summer

House
1. It's ____big____.

Game
2. It's ________.

Uncle
3. He's ________.

Cousin
4. She's ________.

E **Look at D. Write sentences. Use *he's*, *she's*, or *it's*.**

回顾上一题，用he's、she's 或it's 完成句子。

1. 

This is my grandparents' house.

____It's____ big.

2. 

This is a game.

________ fun.

3. 

This is my uncle.

________ tall.

4. 

This is my cousin.

________ pretty.

MY LISTENING GOALS

☐ **I can listen to the presentation.** 我能听懂这场课堂展示。

☐ **I can listen for answers.** 我能听清答案。

UNITS

7 and 8

Listening Check

Remember!
Listen for **questions**. What do they ask?
Listen for **answers**. What do they tell you?
注意听问题问了什么。问题后面的答案传达了什么信息？

A Listen to the conversation *Apple Farm*. Choose the correct picture. 听一听这段对话，并选择相应的图片。

A ☐

B ☐

C ☐

B What questions are in the conversation? Choose ✔ or ✘.
对话中提了哪些问题？根据听到的内容判断正误。

1. Who is John? ✔ ✘
2. Is he tall? ✔ ✘
3. Where are your parents? ✔ ✘
4. Do you have apples? ✔ ✘

C What answers are in the conversation? Choose ✔ or ✘.
对话中问题的答案是什么？根据听到的内容判断正误。

1. He's my brother. ✔ ✘
2. No, he isn't. He's short. ✔ ✘
3. Yes, he is. He has a blue cap. ✔ ✘
4. Yes, I have 10 apples! ✔ ✘

D Listen to *Apple Farm* again. Choose the correct answer.

再听一听对话，并选择正确的答案。

1. How many boys are there?

   ☐ a. Two. ☑ b. Three. ☐ c. Four.

2. Who is John?

   ☐ a. A cousin. ☐ b. An uncle. ☐ c. A parent.

3. What does John have?

   ☐ a. A red shirt. ☐ b. A blue car. ☐ c. A blue cap.

4. Where is John?

   ☐ a. Under the tree. ☐ b. On the chair. ☐ c. By the table.

5. How many apples does John have?

   ☐ a. 12. ☐ b. 20. ☐ c. 10.

E Listen to *Apple Farm* again. Complete the sentences.

再听一听对话，并补全句子。

Three (1) ___boys___ are at an apple farm.

Chris: Where is John?

Todd: Who is John?

Chris: He's my (2) ________.

Todd: There are some (3) ________. I see a boy. Is he tall?

Chris: Yes, he is. He has a blue cap.

Todd: He's with your (4) ________! He's under the tree.

Chris: John! Do you have apples?

John: Yes, I have 10 apples!

UNITS 7 and 8

Get Ready to Speak

SPEAKING GOAL: Ask Questions to Find Information

口语训练目标：通过问问题获取信息

Questions help you get information. They help you find out about a person, place, or thing. 问问题能帮你获取信息，了解某人、某地或者某物。

A Read and listen to the conversation. Underline the question words.

读一读，听一听，在疑问词下面画横线。

Speaking Tip

Use question words like *who*, *what*, or *how* to find information.

用who、what或者how等疑问词引导的句子提问，获取更多信息。

Lily: Who is this?

Justin: This is my cousin.

Lily: Where does he live?

Justin: He lives in Canada.

Lily: How old is he?

Justin: He's 11 years old.

B Look at **A**. What are the questions? Complete the diagram.

回顾上一题，对话中提了哪些问题？完成思维导图。

My Cousin

Questions		Answers
1. Who is this?	→	This is my cousin.
2. ________	→	He lives in Canada.
3. ________	→	He's 11 years old.

Speak

C Think about someone in your family. Complete the diagram.

想一想你的某个家人，完成思维导图。

My ________________

Questions		Answers
________________	→	________________
________________	→	________________
________________	→	________________

D Draw the person. Then write about the person. Use your ideas from **C**. Choose new words, too.

顺着上一题的思路，介绍一下这个人，然后把他画出来。

This is my ________________.

He / She ________________.

He's / She's ________________.

Look at your partner's picture. Then ask questions about your partner's picture. What do you find out about the person?

看看你的小伙伴画了谁，根据他画的画问一些问题。通过他的回答，你了解了关于这个人的哪些信息?

MY SPEAKING GOAL

☐ I can ask questions to find information.

我会通过问问题获取信息。

TOPIC

5 Likes and Dislikes

SOCIAL STUDIES

MY GOALS

UNIT 9

- Listen to the story *Teddy Bear and Bird*
- Listen for likes

UNIT 10

- Listen to the passage *Pete and Mia*
- Listen for dislikes

SPEAK

- Describe likes and dislikes

A **Look at the picture. What do you see?**
看图片，回答问题。

1. Are the people happy or sad?
2. Where do you go for fun?

FUN FACT

Listen

A Roller Coaster

B **Listen to the Fun Fact. Then answer the questions.** 听“奇闻趣事”，回答问题。

1. Is it long or short? Is it fast or slow?
2. Can you ride a roller coaster?
   Do you like it? Why or why not?

Think, Pair, Share
What do you like to ride?
你喜欢乘坐什么游乐设施?

UNIT 9

Get Ready to Listen

Let's learn the **key words**.
一起来学习重点词汇吧！

A Listen, point, and say. Write the words in your picture dictionary.

听一听，指一指，说一说。在“图解词典”中写出对应的单词。

bike

boat

scooter

teddy bear

B Listen and color. 听一听，涂一涂。

C Listen and write. 听一听，写一写。

1. ______boat______
2. ____________
3. ____________
4. ____________

Listen

LISTENING GOAL: Listen for Likes 听力训练目标：明确喜好

Likes are things people think are good. Listen for likes to know how people feel about things.
人们喜好的事物是人们觉得好因而喜欢的东西。注意听人们喜欢什么，了解人们对事物的态度。

A **Listen. Then complete the sentences.** 听一听，并补全句子。

1. The girl likes the ____ball____.
2. The boy likes to ride on the ________.
3. She likes the ________.

Teddy Bear and Bird

B **Listen to the story *Teddy Bear and Bird*. What is it about? Choose the correct picture.**
听一听这个故事讲了什么内容，并选择相应的图片。

A

☐

B

☐

Now put the sentences in order. 给句子排序。

a. They go on a boat. ☐
b. Teddy Bear rides a bike. 1
c. Bird flies up. ☐

What does Bird **like**?
小鸟喜欢什么？

Think!
What toys do you like?
你喜欢什么玩具？

Understand

A **Think about *Teddy Bear and Bird*. What does Teddy Bear like?**
回想一下故事，泰迪熊喜欢什么？

☐ a. The bike.
☐ b. The scooter.

Remember!
Likes tell how people feel about things.
人们对事物的感受能体现人们的态度。

B **Listen to *Teddy Bear and Bird* again. Choose the correct answer.**
再听一听故事，圈出正确的答案。

1. Teddy Bear has a **ball** / **balloon**.
2. The bike is **big** / **little**.
3. The scooter is **little** / **big**.
4. The boat is **old** / **fast**.
5. Bird **gets** / **doesn't get** the balloon.

C **Listen. Complete each sentence with a key word. Then match.**
听一听，用本单元的重点词汇补全句子，并与相应的图片配对。

1. I see a blue ___boat___.
2. He rides a __________.
3. Is this your __________?
4. She has a new __________.

a. ____ 

b. ____ 

c. __1__ 

d. ____ 

D Listen to *Teddy Bear and Bird* again. What does Teddy Bear like? What does Bird like? Complete the diagram.

再听一听故事，泰迪熊喜欢什么？小鸟喜欢什么？完成思维导图。

Likes

- **Teddy Bear**
  1. Teddy Bear likes his new __balloon__.
  2. He likes the ________.
  3. He likes this ________.
- **Bird**
  4. She likes the ________.

E Look at D. Write. Use *like* or *likes*. 回顾上一题，用like或likes完成句子。

1\. 

He __likes__ his new balloon. It's fun!

2\. 

He ________ the bike. It's big.

3\. 

"I ________ this boat," says Teddy Bear.

4\. 

She ________ the scooter. It's little.

MY LISTENING GOALS

- [ ] **I can listen to the story.** 我能听懂这个故事。
- [ ] **I can listen for likes.** 我知道人们喜欢哪些事物。

Get Ready to Listen

Let's learn the **key words**.
一起来学习重点词汇吧！

A Listen, point, and say. Write the words in your picture dictionary.

听一听，指一指，说一说。在“图解词典”中写出对应的单词。

carrots

mango

peach

tomato

B Listen and number. 听一听，在圆圈里填上正确的序号。

C Listen and complete the sentences. 听一听，并补全句子。

1. The ___carrots___ are on the table.
2. He eats the ________.
3. I don't have a ________.
4. Where is the ________?

Listen

LISTENING GOAL: Listen for Dislikes 听力训练目标：明确嫌恶

Dislikes are things people think are bad. Listen for dislikes to know how people feel about things. 人们嫌恶的事物是人们觉得不好因而不喜欢的东西。注意听人们不喜欢什么，了解人们对事物的态度。

A **Listen. Is the picture correct? Choose ✔ or ✘.**
听一听，图片是否准确描述了你听到的内容？判断正误。

1. 

✔ ✘

2. 
✔ ✘

3. 
✔ ✘

Pete and Mia

B **Listen to the passage *Pete and Mia*. What is it about? Choose the correct picture.**
听一听这篇文章讲了什么内容，并选择相应的图片。

A

B

Now choose ✔ or ✘. 判断正误。

1. Pete and Mia are thirsty. ✔ ✘
2. Mia doesn't like the salad. ✔ ✘
3. Pete and Mia have mango juice. ✔ ✘

Does Mia like carrots?
米娅喜欢吃胡萝卜吗？

Think!
What foods do you like? What foods don't you like?
你喜欢吃什么，不喜欢吃什么？

Understand

A Think about *Pete and Mia*. What doesn't Mia like? Choose the correct answer.

回想一下文章，米娅不喜欢吃什么？选择正确的答案。

☐ a. Fish. ☐ b. Tomatoes.

Remember!
People sometimes say what they **don't like**. Listen for these words.
人们有时候会讲到自己不喜欢的东西，注意听相关的单词。

B Listen to *Pete and Mia* again. Choose the correct answer.

再听一听文章，选择正确的答案。

1. What is in the salad?
   ☐ a. Eggs. ☑ b. Carrots.
2. What does Mia like?
   ☐ a. Peaches. ☐ b. Pizza.
3. How do Pete and Mia feel?
   ☐ a. Sad. ☐ b. Happy.

C Listen and choose the correct picture. Then write the key word.

听一听，选择恰当的图片，并将相应的词写在下方的横线上。

1.

☑ a

☐ b

tomato

2.

☐ a

☐ b

____

3.

☐ a

☐ b

____

4.

☐ a

☐ b

____

D Listen to *Pete and Mia* again. What doesn't Mia like? Complete the diagram.

再听一听文章，米娅不喜欢什么？完成思维导图。

Dislikes

1. She doesn't like ____carrots____.
2. She doesn't like ________.
3. She doesn't like the ________.
4. Mia doesn't like ________.

E Look at D. Write. Use *don't like* or *doesn't like*.

回顾上一题，用don't like或doesn't like完成句子。

1. 

I ____don't like____ carrots.

2. 

I ________ tomatoes.

3. 

She ________ the salad.

4. 

Mia ________ mangoes.

MY LISTENING GOALS

- [ ] **I can listen to the passage.** 我能听懂这篇文章。
- [ ] **I can listen for dislikes.** 我知道人们不喜欢哪些事物。

UNITS
9 and 10

Listening Check

Remember!
Listen for **likes** and **dislikes**. How do people feel about things?
注意听人们喜欢什么、不喜欢什么。人们对事物的态度是什么样的?

A Listen to the story *What Do You Like?*. Choose the correct picture.

听一听这个故事，并选择相应的图片。

☐

☐

☐

B What do Jake and Ben like? Choose ✔ or ✘.

杰克和本分别喜欢什么？根据听到的内容判断正误。

1. Jake likes bikes. ✔ (✘)
2. Jake likes carrots. ✔ ✘
3. Ben likes peaches. ✔ ✘
4. Ben likes chicken. ✔ ✘

C What do Jake and Ben *not* like? Choose ✔ or ✘.

杰克和本分别不喜欢什么？根据听到的内容判断正误。

1. Ben doesn't like scooters. (✔) ✘
2. Jake doesn't like scooters. ✔ ✘
3. Ben doesn't like carrots. ✔ ✘
4. Jake doesn't like chicken. ✔ ✘

D **Listen to *What Do You Like?* again. Choose the correct answer.**

再听一听故事，并选择正确的答案。

1. What do Jake and Ben do?

   ☑ a. Play. ☐ b. Read. ☐ c. Dance.

2. Who has a scooter?

   ☐ a. Jake. ☐ b. Ben. ☐ c. Lee.

3. Who has a bike?

   ☐ a. Jake. ☐ b. Ben. ☐ c. Lee.

4. How do Jake and Ben feel?

   ☐ a. Sad. ☐ b. Hungry. ☐ c. Thirsty.

5. What does Ben's mom have?

   ☐ a. Chicken. ☐ b. Sandwiches. ☐ c. Cake.

E **Listen to *What Do You Like?* again. Complete the sentences.**

再听一听故事，并补全句子。

Jake and Ben play outdoors.

"I like my (1) __scooter__. It's fast!" says Jake.

But Ben doesn't like scooters.

They're little.

Ben likes (2) __________!

Jake and Ben are hungry.

"I like (3) __________," says Jake.

But Ben doesn't like carrots.

He likes (4) __________.

"Boys!" says Ben's mom. "Do you want chicken?"

They like chicken! They go!

UNITS 9 and 10

Get Ready to Speak

SPEAKING GOAL: Describe Likes and Dislikes

口语训练目标：表达喜好和嫌恶

Likes are things you feel good about. Dislikes are things you do not like.
你喜好的事物是你觉得好且喜欢的东西，你嫌恶的事物是你觉得不好且不喜欢的东西。

A **Read and listen to the conversation. Underline *and* and *but*.**
读一读，听一听，在对话中的and和but下面画横线。

Speaking Tip
Use *and* and *but* to talk about likes and dislikes.
在表达喜好和嫌恶的时候，可以用and和but。

Karam: I like video games, but I don't like books. What do you like?

Beth: I like puppets. Do you like fruit?

Karam: Yes, I like mangoes and bananas.

Beth: I like mangoes, but I don't like bananas.

B **Look at A. What do Karam and Beth like? What don't they like? Complete the diagram.** 回顾上一题，卡拉姆和贝丝分别喜欢什么、不喜欢什么？完成思维导图。

Karam

Likes
1. video games
2. ______
3. ______

Dislikes
4. ______

Beth

Likes
5. ______
6. ______

Dislikes
7. ______

Speak

C **Think. What do you like? What don't you like? Complete the diagram.**
想一想，你喜欢什么、不喜欢什么？完成思维导图。

My name: ____________________

Likes	Dislikes
____________________	____________________
____________________	____________________

D **Now work with your partner. Write about your likes and dislikes. Use your ideas from C. Choose new words, too. Then draw one like and one dislike.**
顺着上一题的思路，和小伙伴一起写一写你们喜欢的事物和不喜欢的事物，然后分别画一画它们。

Me: I like ____________, but I don't like ____________. What do you like?

My partner: I like ____________.
Do you like ____________?

Me: Yes, I like ____________
and ____________.

My partner: I like ____________,
but I don't like ____________.

Say your conversation with your partner. Talk about your likes and dislikes.
和小伙伴聊一聊你们各自喜欢什么、不喜欢什么。

MY SPEAKING GOAL

☐ **I can talk about likes and dislikes.**
我能讲出自己喜欢什么、不喜欢什么。

TOPIC 6

HEALTH

My Face and Body

MY GOALS

UNIT 11

- Listen to the story *Tim Tiger and Friends*
- Listen for characters and names

UNIT 12

- Listen to the conversation *Funny Face*
- Listen for the speaker

SPEAK

- Describe a favorite activity

A **Look at the picture. What do you see?**
看图片，回答问题。

1. What can the girl do?
2. Do you do this? Do you like it? Why or why not?

FUN FACT

Listen

Up, Up, Up!

B **Listen to the Fun Fact. Then answer the questions.** 听“奇闻趣事”，回答问题。

1. What does the girl use to climb?
2. What can you do with your hands and feet?

Think, Pair, Share
What do you like to do outdoors?
你喜欢参加什么户外运动?

UNIT 11

Get Ready to Listen

Let's learn the **key words.**
一起来学习重点词汇吧！

A Listen, point, and say. Write the words in your picture dictionary.

听一听，指一指，说一说。在“图解词典”中写出对应的单词。

body

head

legs

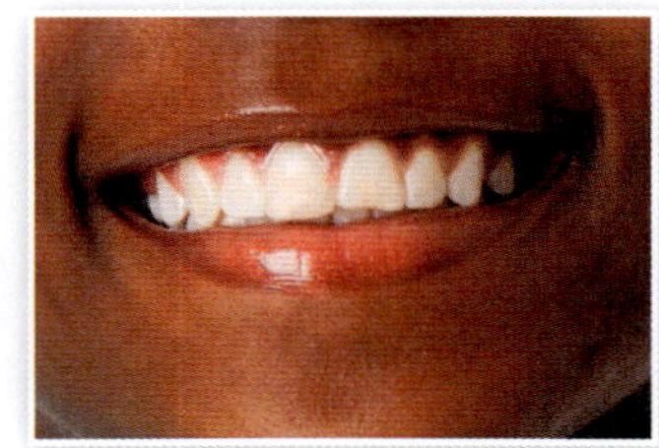

teeth

B Listen and color. 听一听，涂一涂。

C Listen and write. 听一听，写一写。

1. legs ____________
2. ____________
3. ____________
4. ____________

Listen

LISTENING GOAL: Listen for Characters and Names

听力训练目标：明确人物和名字

Some stories are about people or animals. Listen for names of characters. They tell who is in the story. 有的故事是关于人的，有的故事是关于动物的。注意听人物的名字，名字能告诉我们故事中都有谁。

A **Listen. Then complete the sentences.** 听一听，并补全句子。

1. Harry is a lion.
2. The two hands are __________'s.
3. The girl's name is __________.

Tim Tiger and Friends

B **Listen to the story *Tim Tiger and Friends*. What is it about? Choose the correct picture.**

听一听这个故事讲了什么内容，并选择相应的图片。

A

☐

B

☐

Now put the sentences in order. 给句子排序。

a. Tim Tiger is in the triangle. ☐

b. The mouse and the hen help. ☐

c. Tim Tiger jumps. 1

Who are the **characters**?
故事中都有谁?

Think!

Who are your favorite characters from stories?
你最喜欢的故事人物是谁?

Understand

A Think about *Tim Tiger and Friends*. Who is in the story?

回想一下故事，里面都有谁？

- ☐ a. Tim, Peter, and Max.
- ☐ b. Tim, Max, and Heidi.

Remember!
Listen for **names**. Names tell who the characters are.
注意听人物的名字，名字能告诉我们故事中都有谁。

B Listen to *Tim Tiger and Friends* again. Choose the correct answer.

再听一听故事，圈出正确的答案。

1. Tim Tiger has a big **arm** / **head**.
2. He has long **legs** / **ears**.
3. The mouse has a **little** / **big** triangle.
4. Heidi pulls **Tim** / **Max**.
5. Tim Tiger has **little** / **big** teeth.

C Listen. Complete each sentence with a key word. Then match.

听一听，用本单元的重点词汇补全句子，并与相应的图片配对。

1. We have two ___legs___.
2. I brush my ________.
3. I can touch my ________.
4. This is my ________.

a. ____

b. ____

c. ____

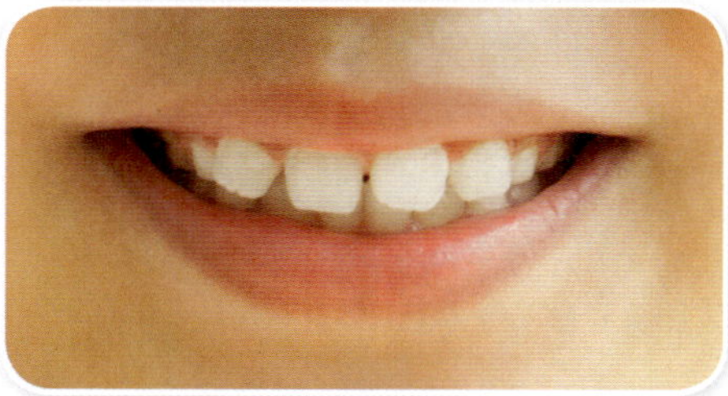

d. __1__

D Listen to *Tim Tiger and Friends* again. What does Tim Tiger have? Complete the table.

再听一听故事，老虎蒂姆的身体部位是什么样的？完成表格。

	long	big
1. head		✔
2. body		
3. legs		
4. teeth		

E Look at D. Complete the sentences. Use *long* or *big*.

回顾上一题，用long或big完成句子。

1. 

He has a ____big____ head.

2. 

He has a ________ body.

3 

He has ________ legs.

4. 

He has ________ teeth.

MY LISTENING GOALS

☐ **I can listen to the story.** 我能听懂这个故事。

☐ **I can listen for characters and names.** 我知道故事中有哪些人物，还知道人物的名字。

UNIT 12

Get Ready to Listen

A **Listen, point, and say. Write the words in your picture dictionary.**
听一听，指一指，说一说。在“图解词典”中写出对应的单词。

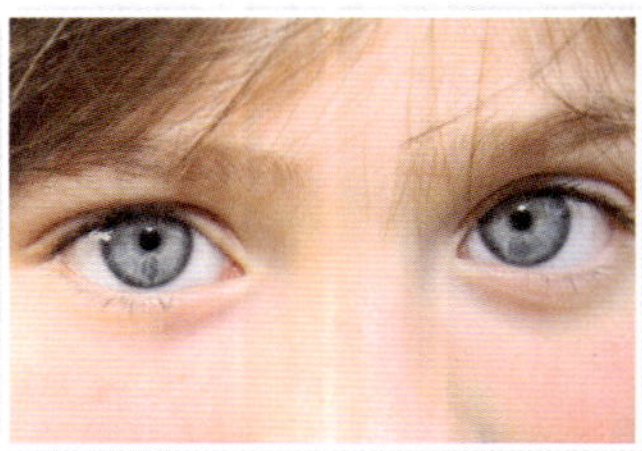

eyes

face

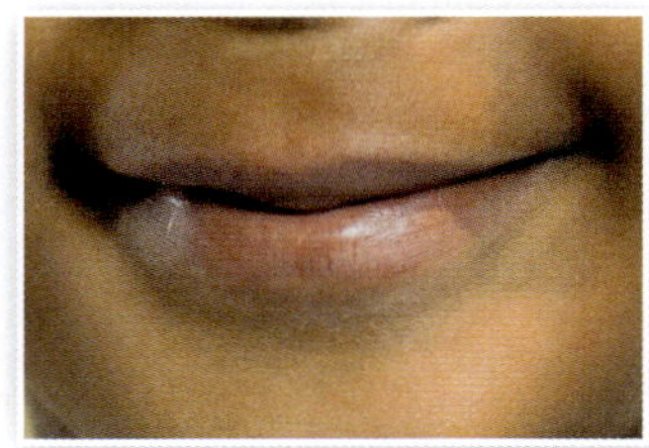

mouth

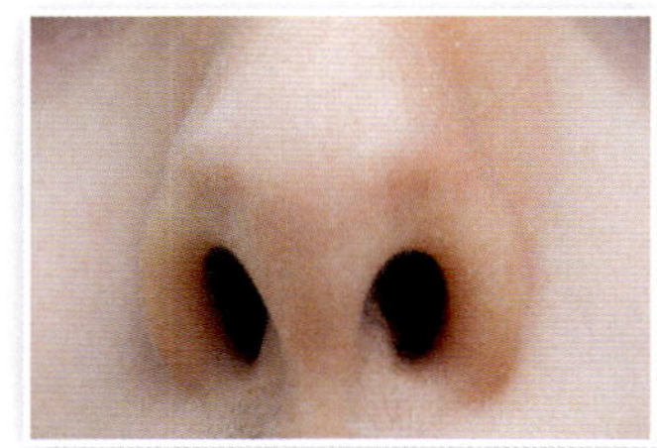

nose

B **Listen and number.** 听一听，在圆圈里填上正确的序号。

C **Listen and complete the sentences.** 听一听，并补全句子。

1. My ___face___ is little and round.
2. I can touch my ________.
3. I have a long ________.
4. This is my ________.

Listen

LISTENING GOAL: Listen for the Speaker 听力训练目标：明确讲话者是谁

The speaker is the person talking. There can be many speakers. Names tell who the speakers are. 讲话者就是说话的人。在一段录音中，可能有多位讲话者。名字能告诉我们是谁在说话。

A Listen. Are the speakers' names correct? Choose ✔ or ✘.

听一听，录音中的讲话者与图片上的名字是否相符？判断正误。

1. Sally

✔ ✘

2. Cora Kenny

✔ ✘

3. Julie Kazu

✔ ✘

Funny Face

B Listen to the conversation *Funny Face*. What is it about? Choose the correct picture.

听一听这段对话讲了什么内容，并选择相应的图片。

A

☐

B

☐

Now choose ✔ or ✘. 判断正误。

1. Anna makes a pizza. ✔ ✘
2. Mike helps. ✔ ✘
3. They make a face. ✔ ✘

Who are the **speakers**?
讲话者都有谁？

Think! What can you make with fruit?
你能用水果做什么？

Understand

A Think about *Funny Face*. Who are the speakers? Choose Yes or No.

回想一下对话，里面的讲话者都有谁？判断正误。

1. Anna and Mike. **Yes** **No**
2. Jacob and Anna. **Yes** **No**

Remember!
Listen for **names**.
Who speaks?
注意听名字，是谁在说话？

B Listen to *Funny Face* again. Choose the correct answer.

再听一听对话，选择正确的答案。

1. What does Anna have?
   - ☐ a. Cherries.
   - ☑ b. A banana.
2. What does Mike have?
   - ☐ a. Apples.
   - ☐ b. Cherries.
3. What does Anna make?
   - ☐ a. A nose.
   - ☐ b. Eyes.

C Listen and choose the correct picture. Then write the key word.

听一听，选择恰当的图片，并将相应的词写在下方的横线上。

1.

☑ a

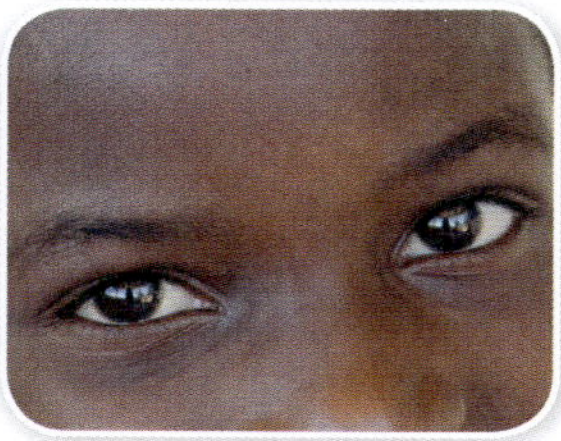

☐ b

face

2.

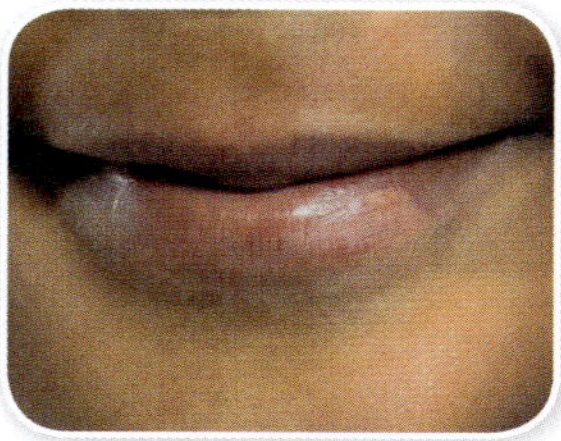

☐ a

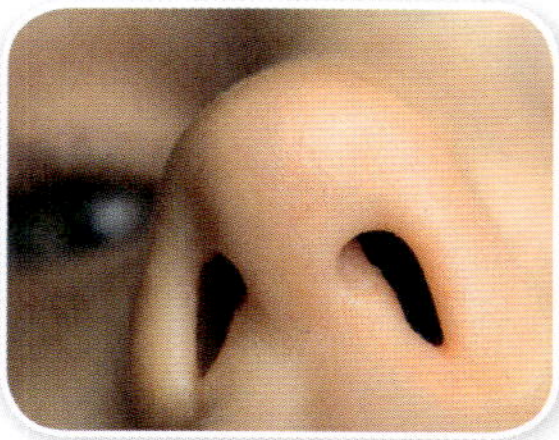

☐ b

____

3.

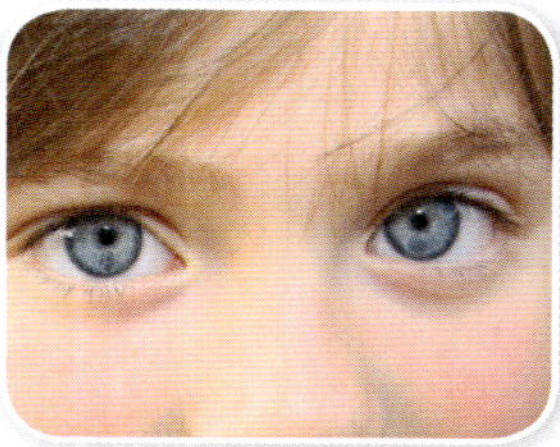

☐ a

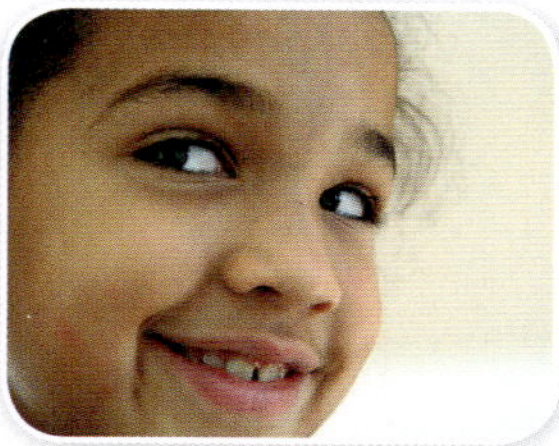

☐ b

____

4.

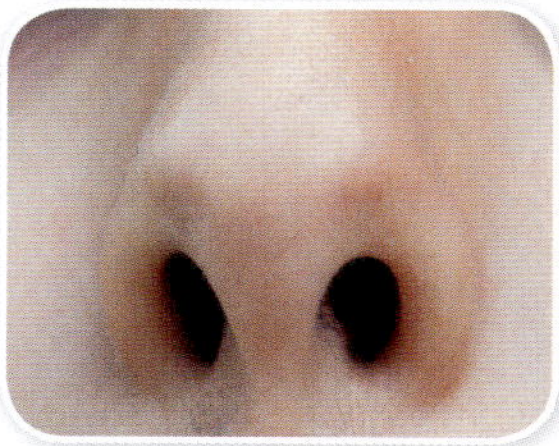

☐ a

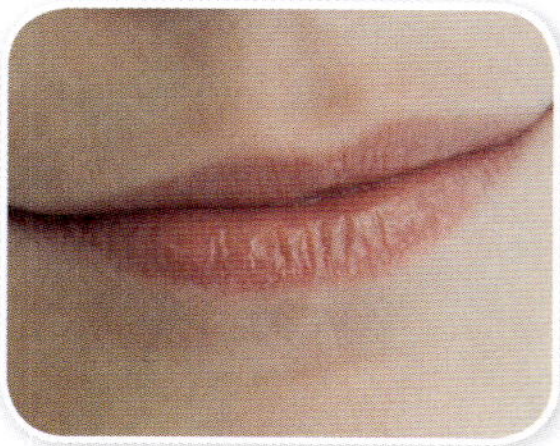

☐ b

____

D Listen to ***Funny Face*** again. What can Anna do? What can Mike do? Complete the diagram. 再听一听对话，安娜可以做什么？迈克可以做什么？完成思维导图。

- **What can you do?**
  - **Anna** I can make
    - 1. a mouth
    - 2. ______
  - **Mike** I can make
    - 3. ______

E Look and read. Write sentences. Use *can make*. 看一看，读一读，用can make回答问题。

1.

What can she do?

She can make a cake.

2.

What can she do?

______

3.

What can she do?

______

4.

What can she do?

______

MY LISTENING GOALS

- ☐ I can listen to the conversation. 我能听懂这段对话。
- ☐ I can listen for the speaker. The speaker is the person who talks. 我能听出是谁在说话。

UNITS **11 and 12**

Listening Check

Remember!
Listen for **characters** and **names**. Who is the story about? Listen for the **speaker**. Who talks?
注意听人物和名字。这个故事是关于谁的？注意听是谁在说话。

A Listen to the story *What Is It?*. Choose the correct picture.
听一听这个故事，并选择相应的图片。

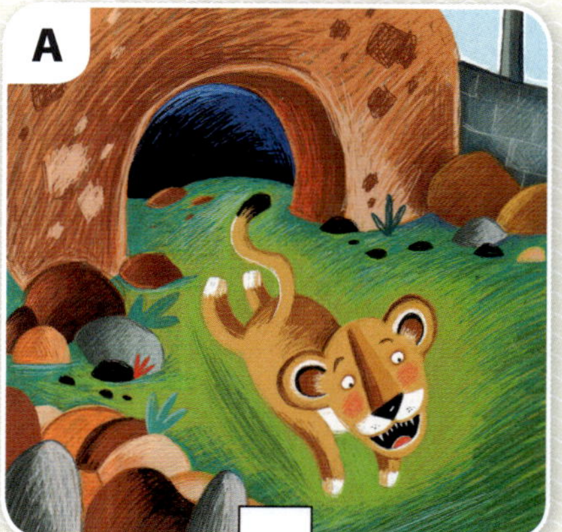

☐

☐

☐

B Who are the characters? Choose ✔ or ✘.
故事中的人物都有谁？根据听到的内容判断正误。

1. Lucy. ✔ ✘
2. Emma. ✔ ✘
3. Shoma. ✔ ✘
4. Maya. ✔ ✘

C Listen to *What Is It?* again. Who is the speaker? Choose the correct answer.
再听一听故事，下面的话分别是谁说的？圈出正确的答案。

1. "I see something!" Lucy Shoma
2. "What is it?" Lucy Maya
3. "It has little teeth!" Maya Shoma
4. "It has short legs!" Shoma Maya

D Listen to *What Is It?* again. Choose the correct answer.

再听一听故事，并选择正确的答案。

1. Where are the friends?
   - [ ] a. At the park.
   - [ ] b. By the flowers.
   - [x] c. At the zoo.
2. What does the animal have?
   - [ ] a. A big nose.
   - [ ] b. Big teeth.
   - [ ] c. Long legs.
3. What does the animal have?
   - [ ] a. Round eyes.
   - [ ] b. Blue eyes.
   - [ ] c. Green eyes.
4. What is the animal?
   - [ ] a. A baby frog.
   - [ ] b. A baby bird.
   - [ ] c. A baby lion.
5. What does the animal do?
   - [ ] a. It runs.
   - [ ] b. It jumps.
   - [ ] c. It climbs.

E Listen to *What Is It?* again. Complete the sentences.

再听一听故事，并补全句子。

Lucy, Shoma, and Maya are at the zoo.

"I see something!" says Shoma.

"What is it?" asks Lucy.

"I don't know."

"It has a big (1) __nose__ !" says Maya.

"It has little (2) ________ !" says Shoma.

"It has round (3) ________ !" says Lucy.

"It has short (4) ________ !" says Maya.

It's a baby lion!

The lion jumps.

UNITS
11 and 12

Get Ready to Speak

SPEAKING GOAL: Describe a Favorite Activity

口语训练目标：描述你最喜欢的活动

An activity is something you do. You can give a description of an activity. You can say where you do it. You can also say how you feel about it.

活动就是你做的事情。描述一下你喜欢做的事情，可以讲一讲你喜欢在哪里做这件事以及有什么感受。

A Read and listen to the passage *My Favorite Activity*. Underline *I'm* and *It's*.

读一读，听一听，在文章中的I'm和It's下面画横线。

Speaking Tip

I am = I'm. It is = It's. Use *I'm* and *It's* in your description about your activity.

在英语中，I am=I'm，It is=It's。描述你喜欢做的事情时，可以用这些简写形式。

My Favorite Activity

I like soccer. It's fun.
I play in the park. It's big.
I'm happy.

B Look at **A**. What does the speaker say? Complete the diagram.

回顾上一题，讲话者说了什么？完成思维导图。

My Favorite Activity

- What is it?
  1. soccer
- Where do you do it?
  2. ____________
- How do you feel?
  3. ____________

Speak

C Think about your favorite activity. Complete the diagram.

想一想你最喜欢做的事情是什么，并完成思维导图。

My Favorite Activity

- What is it? ______
- Where do you do it? ______
- How do you feel? ______

D Now write about your favorite activity. Use your ideas from **C**. Choose new words, too. Then draw your activity.

顺着上一题的思路，写一写你最喜欢做的事情，然后画一幅与这件事相关的画。

I like ______.

It's ______.

I ______ in / at ______.

It's ______.

I'm ______.

Talk about your favorite activity with your partner.

和小伙伴讲一讲你最喜欢做的事情。

MY SPEAKING GOAL

☐ I can describe my favorite activity.

我会描述我最喜欢做的事情。

Listening WITH Speaking 1

Workbook

WORKBOOK
UNIT
1

Listen

LISTENING GOAL:
Listen for the Title
听力训练目标：听清标题

Remember!
The **title** tells what the listening is about. It's at the beginning.
标题在开头出现，能告诉我们听力材料是关于什么的。

A **Listen to the story *A Friend for Duck*. What is it about? Choose ✔ or ✘.**
听一听这个故事讲了什么，并判断正误。

1. 

A duck and a mouse. ☐✔ ☐✘

2. 

A duck and a cow. ☐✔ ☐✘

B **Think about *A Friend for Duck*. What does the title tell you about the story? Choose ✔ or ✘.** 回想一下故事，标题告诉了你什么？判断正误。

1. Duck wants a friend. ☐✔ ☐✘
2. Duck has a ball. ☐✔ ☐✘
3. There is an animal in the story. ☐✔ ☐✘

C **Listen to *A Friend for Duck* again. Choose the correct answer.**
再听一听故事，选择正确的答案。

1. Who helps Duck?
   ☐ a. Duck.　☑ b. Cow.　☐ c. Mouse.
2. Where are the animals?
   ☐ a. At the park.　☐ b. At the zoo.　☐ c. At the farm.
3. What does Duck see?
   ☐ a. A sheep.　☐ b. A tree.　☐ c. A bee.
4. How many little ducks are there?
   ☐ a. 2.　☐ b. 10.　☐ c. 12.

D Listen and write the word. Then choose the correct picture.

听一听，写出正确的单词，并选择相应的图片。

1. duck

☐ a

☑ b

2. ______

☐ a

☐ b

3. ______

☐ a

☐ b

4. ______

☐ a

☐ b

E Complete the sentences. 选一选，填一填（每个选项限用一次）。

duck	sheep	~~cow~~	monkey

1. We drink milk from the cow.
2. The ______ can climb.
3. A ______ can fly.
4. A ______ can eat grass all day.

F Unscramble and write. 理一理，写出正确的单词。

1. k u d c

   duck

2. p h e s e

   ______

3. o y e k m n

   ______

4. o c w

   ______

WORKBOOK
UNIT
2

Listen

LISTENING GOAL:
Listen for the Topic
听力训练目标：明确话题

Remember!
The **topic** is what the listening is about. Look at the **title** and **pictures**. They can tell you the topic.
话题告诉我们听力材料是关于什么的。标题和图片有助于你明确话题。

A Listen to the conversation *City Zoo*. Then put the pictures in order.

听一听这段对话，给图片排序。

A

☐

B

☐

C

1

B Think about *City Zoo*. What is the topic? Choose ✔ or ✘.

回想一下对话，它的话题是什么？判断正误。

1. Don has an apple. ✔ ✘
2. Amy and Don have fun at the zoo. ✔ ✘
3. The zoo is too big. ✔ ✘

C Listen to *City Zoo* again. Choose Yes or No.

再听一听对话，判断正误。

1. Amy is hot. Yes No
2. There are seven crocodiles. Yes No
3. The elephant is under the tree. Yes No
4. Don and Amy see a giraffe. Yes No
5. Don is hungry. Yes No
6. There is a bee on the apple. Yes No

D Listen. Then read and choose the correct answer.

听一听，读一读，并选择正确的答案。

1. What does the girl see?

a. 
b. 
c. 

2. What is at the zoo?

a. 
b. 
c. 

3. What is old?

a. 
b. 
c. 

E Complete the sentences. 根据首字母提示，用本单元的重点词汇补全句子。

1. The ______elephant______ is big.
2. The m______________ is little.
3. The g______________ is tall.
4. The c______________ is very long.

Speak

Circle *I* and *my*. 把I和my圈出来。

I am 7 years old.

Jean is my friend.

I like my new game.

Remember!
Use *I* and *my* to give an introduction.
做自我介绍时可以使用代词I和my。

WORKBOOK

UNIT

3

Listen

LISTENING GOAL:
Listen for Numbers
听力训练目标：听清数词

A Listen to the conversation *A Robot*. What is it about? Choose ✔ or ✘.

听一听这段对话讲了什么，并判断正误。

1. 

A paper robot. ✔ ✘

2. 

A book. ✔ ✘

B Think about *A Robot*. Are the numbers correct? Choose ✔ or ✘.

回想一下对话，下列句子中关于数量的表述正确吗？判断正误。

1. There is one heart. ✔ ✘
2. There are two squares. ✔ ✘
3. There are three rectangles. ✔ ✘

C Listen to *A Robot* again. Choose the correct answer.

再听一听对话，选择正确的答案。

1. Who has paper?
   - [✔] a. Min-Jun.
   - [ ] b. Sue.
   - [ ] c. Ella.
2. What color are the squares?
   - [ ] a. White.
   - [ ] b. Brown.
   - [ ] c. Gray.
3. What color are the rectangles?
   - [ ] a. Gray.
   - [ ] b. Brown.
   - [ ] c. Purple.
4. What color is the heart?
   - [ ] a. Orange.
   - [ ] b. Pink.
   - [ ] c. Purple.

D **Listen and write the word. Then choose the correct picture.**
听一听，写出正确的单词，并选择相应的图片。

1. ______ white ______

☑ a

☐ b

2. ____________

☐ a

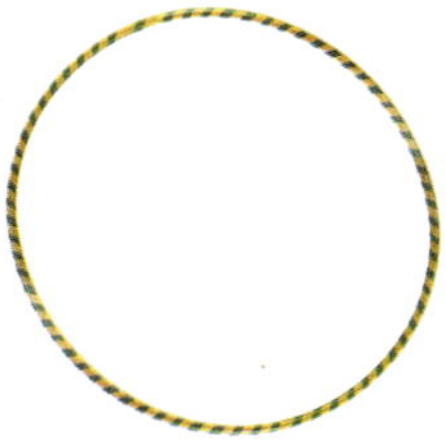
☐ b

3. ____________

☐ a

☐ b

4. ____________

☐ a

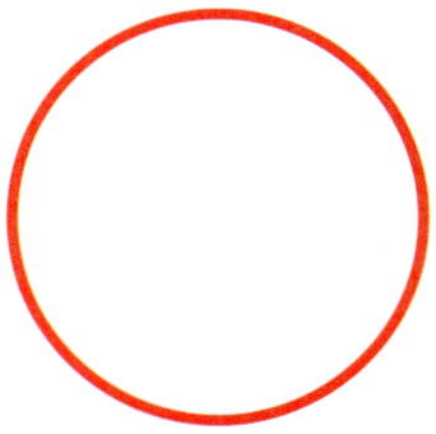
☐ b

E **Complete the sentences.** 选一选，填一填（每个选项限用一次）。

circle	brown	square	~~white~~

1. The snow is ______ white ______.
2. The sun is a ____________.
3. This is a ____________ crayon.
4. It's a ____________ box.

F **Unscramble and write.** 理一理，写出正确的单词。

1. n o r b w

______ brown ______

2. i h e w t

____

3. e l i c r c

____

4. r u s e q a

____

WORKBOOK
UNIT
4

Listen

LISTENING GOAL: Listen for Colors

听力训练目标：听清颜色词

Remember!
Color words tell what color things are.
颜色词能告诉我们东西是什么颜色的。

A **Listen to the story *Ice Cream Juice*. Then put the pictures in order.**
听一听这个故事，给图片排序。

A

1

B

☐

C

☐

B **Think about *Ice Cream Juice*. What are the colors? Choose ✔ or ✘.**
回想一下故事，里面提到了哪些颜色？判断正误。

1. White, red, and blue. ☐✔ ☐✘
2. Blue, red, and brown. ☐✔ ☐✘
3. Red, blue, and green. ☐✔ ☐✘

C **Listen to *Ice Cream Juice* again. Choose Yes or No.**
再听一听故事，判断正误。

1. It's cold today. **Yes** **(No)**
2. Kate has three blue scoops. **Yes** **No**
3. She has two red scoops. **Yes** **No**
4. Kate has orange juice. **Yes** **No**
5. She is hungry. **Yes** **No**
6. Yuki is at the park. **Yes** **No**

D Listen. Then read and choose the correct answer.

听一听，读一读，并选择正确的答案。

1. What color is the umbrella?

a.  b.  (c.) 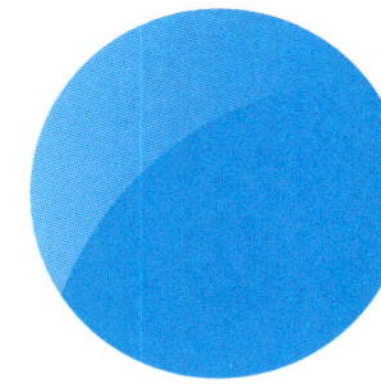

2. What color is the jump rope?

a.  b.  c. 

3. What color is the kite?

a.  b.  c. 

E Complete the sentences. 根据首字母提示，用本单元的重点词汇补全句子。

1. He has a ______blue______ bicycle.
2. I have a y______________ pencil case.
3. The cup is g______________.
4. I see a r______________ bird.

Speak

What words tell about the robot? Circle them. Then tell your partner.

圈出用于描述机器人特征的单词，然后和小伙伴说一说。

This is my robot. It's green. It's little and new.

Remember!

Use color and shape words in your description.

描述时可以使用表示颜色和形状的单词。

WORKBOOK UNIT 5

Listen

LISTENING GOAL:
Listen for Greetings and Endings
听力训练目标：听清问候语和结束语

Remember!
Greetings start a conversation.
Endings stop a conversation.
问候语用于展开对话，结束语用于结束对话。

A Listen to the story *Bob's Day*. What is it about? Choose ✔ or ✘.
听一听这个故事讲了什么，并判断正误。

1. 

Bob has school. ✔ ✘

2. 

Bob can play. ✔ ✘

B Think about *Bob's Day*. What is the greeting? What is the ending? Choose ✔ or ✘.
回想一下故事，里面用了哪些问候语和结束语？判断正误。

1. Hello and thank you. ✔ ✘
2. Hi and see you later. ✔ ✘
3. Hi and goodbye. ✔ ✘

C Listen to *Bob's Day* again. Choose the correct answer.
再听一听故事，选择正确的答案。

1. Where is the pen?
   [✔] a. On the table. [ ] b. Under the bed. [ ] c. On the chair.
2. What does Bob look for?
   [ ] a. A pencil. [ ] b. A notebook. [ ] c. Glue.
3. What does Bob think?
   [ ] a. He is thirsty. [ ] b. He is hungry. [ ] c. He has school.
4. What day is it?
   [ ] a. Sunday. [ ] b. Saturday. [ ] c. Friday.

D Listen and write the word. Then choose the correct picture.

听一听，写出正确的单词，并选择相应的图片。

1. notebook

☑ a

☐ b

2. ______

☐ a

☐ b

3. ______

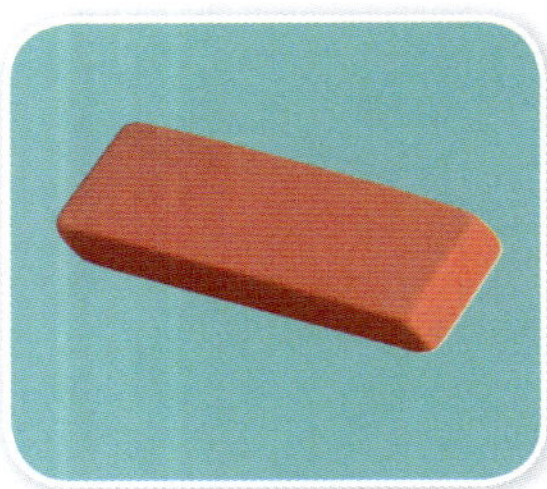
☐ a

☐ b

4. ______

☐ a

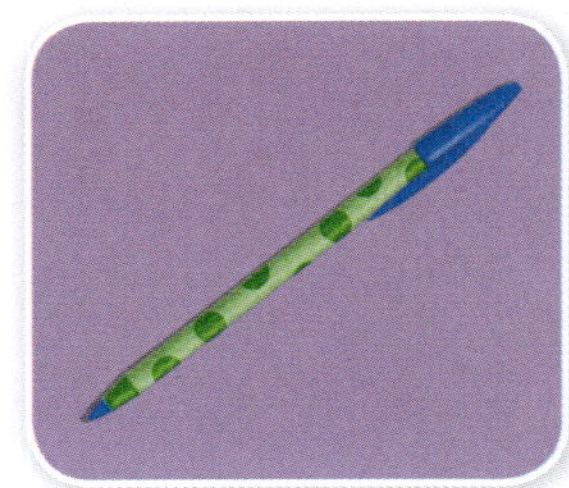
☐ b

E Complete the sentences. 选一选，填一填（每个选项限用一次）。

~~notebook~~	pen	draw	eraser

1. He writes in the notebook.
2. I can ______ a picture.
3. She writes with a ______.
4. The ______ is on the pencil.

F Unscramble and write. 理一理，写出正确的单词。

1. e s a r e r
   eraser
2. n e p
   ______
3. o e k b o n t o
   ______
4. w a d r
   ______

WORKBOOK

UNIT

6

Listen

LISTENING GOAL:

Listen for Key Words

听力训练目标：抓住关键词

Remember!

You can hear some words many times. **Key words** tell what the listening is about.

关键词会出现很多次，关键词能告诉我们听力材料是关于什么的。

A Listen to the presentation *My Picture*. Then put the pictures in order.

听一听这场课堂展示，给图片排序。

[ ]

[1]

[ ]

B Think about *My Picture*. What are the key words? Choose ✔ or ✘.

回想一下课堂展示的内容，里面的关键词是什么？判断正误。

1. paint ✔ ✘
2. scissors ✔ ✘
3. paper ✔ ✘

C Listen to *My Picture* again. Choose Yes or No.

再听一听课堂展示，判断正误。

1. The girl talks about a picture. (Yes) No
2. She is in the park. Yes No
3. The girl has paint. Yes No
4. She uses scissors. Yes No
5. The girl makes a circle. Yes No
6. The boys and girls take out paint. Yes No

D Listen. Then read and choose the correct answer.

听一听，读一读，并选择正确的答案。

1. What does the teacher have?

(a.)  b.  c. 

2. What is on the table?

a.  b.  c. 

3. What is in the bag?

a. 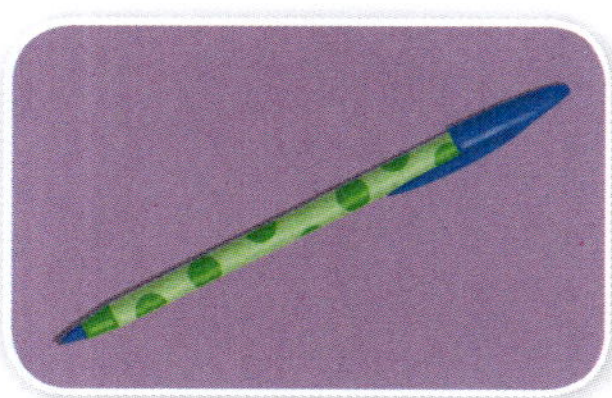 b.  c. 

E Complete the sentences. 根据首字母提示，用本单元的重点词汇补全句子。

1. He puts the pencil in the backpack.
2. I use my r__________ to draw a square.
3. She goes to c__________.
4. He writes on the p__________.

Remember!
Use greetings like *hello* or *hi*.
Use endings like *goodbye* or *see you later*.
用hello和hi之类的问候语展开对话，用goodbye和see you later之类的结束语结束对话。

Speak

Circle the greeting and the ending. Then think of your own greeting and ending. Tell your partner.

把问候语和结束语圈出来。想一想你平时常用哪些问候语和结束语，和小伙伴说一说。

"Hi, I'm Andrew."

"See you later!" says Jane.

WORKBOOK
UNIT
7

Listen

LISTENING GOAL:
Listen for Questions

听力训练目标：听清问题

Remember!
Question words are words like *what*, *where*, or *who*.
Questions ask for information.
英文问句通常由what、where或者who等疑问词引导。问题旨在询问具体信息。

A Listen to the story ***The Snow Family***. What is it about? Choose ✔ or ✘.
听一听这个故事讲了什么，并判断正误。

1. 

A snowman. ☐ ✔ ☐ ✘

2. 

My family. ☐ ✔ ☐ ✘

B Think about ***The Snow Family***. What questions are in the story? Choose ✔ or ✘. 回想一下故事，里面提了哪些问题？判断正误。

1. What is this? ☐ ✔ ☐ ✘
2. Who is the little girl? ☐ ✔ ☐ ✘
3. Where is Sam? ☐ ✔ ☐ ✘

C Listen to ***The Snow Family*** again. Choose the correct answer.
再听一听故事，选择正确的答案。

1. Who is Sam?
   ☐ a. A girl. ☐ b. A parent. ☑ c. A snowman.
2. Who are they?
   ☐ a. Hugo's parents. ☐ b. Sam's parents. ☐ c. Sam's friends.
3. What does the girl do?
   ☐ a. She kicks Sam. ☐ b. She draws a square. ☐ c. She climbs a tree.
4. Where is Sam?
   ☐ a. At the farm. ☐ b. By the school. ☐ c. By the gate.

D Listen and write the word. Then choose the correct picture.

听一听，写出正确的单词，并选择相应的图片。

1. children

☐ a

☑ b

2. ______

☐ a

☐ b

3. ______

☐ a

☐ b

4. ______

☐ a

☐ b

E Complete the sentences. 选一选，填一填（每个选项限用一次）。

children	boy	~~parents~~	girl

1. My parents take me to school.
2. My brother is a ______.
3. The ______ are in the playground.
4. The ______ has a yellow dress.

F Unscramble and write. 理一理，写出正确的单词。

1. y o b

boy

2. e a r n p t s

______

3. l r e h i c n d

______

4. r i g l

______

WORKBOOK UNIT 8

Listen

LISTENING GOAL: Listen for Answers

听力训练目标：听清答案

Remember!
Answers come after questions. Listen for questions. Then listen for the answers.
问题后面会给出答案。注意听问题和问题后面的答案。

A Listen to the conversation *Let's Play!*. Then put the pictures in order.

听一听这段对话，给图片排序。

A

1

B

☐

C

☐

B Think about *Let's Play!*. What answers are in the conversation? Choose ✔ or ✘.

回想一下对话，里面给出了哪些答案？判断正误。

1. I play ball with Jenny. ✔ ✘
2. She's my sister. ✔ ✘
3. I go to the playground. ✔ ✘

C Listen to *Let's Play!* again. Choose Yes or No.

再听一听对话，判断正误。

1. Eva plays ball on Fridays. Yes (No)
2. Jenny is Eva's cousin. Yes No
3. They play at the park. Yes No
4. Eva has chicken. Yes No
5. Eva tells stories. Yes No
6. Jay flies a kite. Yes No

D **Listen. Then read and choose the correct answer.**
听一听，读一读，并选择正确的答案。

1. Who goes to the store?

a.  b.  (c.) 

2. Who likes plums?

a.  b.  c. 

3. Who has a red car?

a.  b.  c. 

E **Complete the sentences.** 根据首字母提示，用本单元的重点词汇补全句子。

1. My ______cousin______ lives on a farm.
2. My u__________________ is a teacher.
3. How many people are there in your f__________________?
4. My g__________________ are 90 years old.

Remember!
Use question words. They are words like *who, what,* or *how*. They help you find information.
用who、what或者how等疑问词引导的句子提问，获取更多信息。

Speak

Circle the question words. Then think of your own questions. Tell your partner.
圈出句子中的疑问词，然后想几个问题，和小伙伴说一说。

Who is she?

Where is this?

WORKBOOK

UNIT

9

Listen

LISTENING GOAL:
Listen for Likes

听力训练目标：明确喜好

Remember!
Likes are things we feel good about.
我们喜好的东西是我们觉得好因而喜欢的东西。

A **Listen to the story *Annie and the Toy*. What is it about? Choose ✔ or ✘.**

听一听这个故事讲了什么，并判断正误。

1. 

A bear on a scooter. ☐ ✔ ☐ ✘

2. 

A teddy bear on a bike. ☐ ✔ ☐ ✘

B **Think about *Annie and the Toy*. What does Annie like? Choose ✔ or ✘.**

回想一下故事，安妮喜欢什么？判断正误。

1. The blue vest. ☐ ✔ ☐ ✘
2. The scooter. ☐ ✔ ☐ ✘
3. The teddy bear. ☐ ✔ ☐ ✘

C **Listen to *Annie and the Toy* again. Choose the correct answer.**

再听一听故事，选择正确的答案。

1. Who is in bed?
   ☐ a. A baby. ☐ b. Ted. ☑ c. Annie.
2. What does Teddy Bear have?
   ☐ a. A vest. ☐ b. A ball. ☐ c. A doll.
3. Where does Annie look?
   ☐ a. On the table. ☐ b. Under the bed. ☐ c. In the box.
4. Where is Teddy Bear?
   ☐ a. On the car. ☐ b. On the book. ☐ c. On the bike.

D Listen and write the word. Then choose the correct picture.

听一听，写出正确的单词，并选择相应的图片。

1. bike

☑ a

☐ b

2. ____________

☐ a

☐ b

3. ____________

☐ a

☐ b

4. ____________

☐ a

☐ b

E Complete the sentences. 选一选，填一填（每个选项限用一次）。

~~teddy bear~~	boat	scooter	bike

1. I like my teddy bear. It's little.
2. The ____________ is in the water.
3. You stand up on a ____________.
4. Teddy Bear rides a ____________.

F Unscramble and write. 理一理，写出正确的单词。

1. r o t o c e s

scooter

2. k i b e

____

3. y e d t d r a b e

____

4. a o t b

____

WORKBOOK

UNIT

10

Listen

LISTENING GOAL:
Listen for Dislikes
听力训练目标：明确嫌恶

Remember!
Dislikes are things we don't feel good about.
我们嫌恶的东西是我们觉得不好因而不喜欢的东西。

A Listen to the passage *A Rainy Day*. Then put the pictures in order.

听一听这篇文章，给图片排序。

1

B Think about *A Rainy Day*. What doesn't Eric like? Choose ✔ or ✘.

回想一下文章，埃里克不喜欢什么？判断正误。

1. Tomatoes. ✔ ✘
2. Tomato juice. ✔ ✘
3. Carrots. ✔ ✘

C Listen to *A Rainy Day* again. Choose ✔ or ✘.

再听一听文章，判断正误。

1. Eric doesn't like rain. ✔ ✘
2. He can go to the park. ✔ ✘
3. Eric is thirsty. ✔ ✘
4. He likes carrot cake. ✔ ✘
5. He plays video games. ✔ ✘
6. It's a bad day. ✔ ✘

D Listen. Then read and choose the correct answer.

听一听，读一读，并选择正确的答案。

1. What does Rita want?

(a.)  b.  c. 

2. What does he put in the box?

a.  b.  c. 

3. What do they get?

a.  b.  c. 

E Complete the sentences. 根据首字母提示，用本单元的重点词汇补全句子。

1. She makes a ___tomato___ sandwich.
2. We can make m________ juice.
3. I can get a p________ from the tree.
4. The c________ are orange.

Remember!
We can use *and* and *but* to talk about likes and dislikes.
在表达喜好和嫌恶的时候，可以用and和but。

Speak

Circle *and* and *but*. Then think of your own sentences with *and* and *but*. Tell your partner.

圈出句子中的 and 和 but，然后用这两个单词造几个句子，和小伙伴说一说。

I like cherries, and I like apples.

I like bananas, but I don't like banana bread.

WORKBOOK
UNIT
11

Listen

LISTENING GOAL:
Listen for Characters and Names
听力训练目标：明确人物和名字

Remember!
Listen for **names** of people or animals. They are the **characters**.
注意听人或者动物的名字，了解故事中都有谁。

A Listen to the story *The Sisters*. What is it about? Choose ✔ or ✘.

听一听这个故事讲了什么，并判断正误。

1. 

Three girls. ✔ ✘

2. 

Two girls. ✔ ✘

B Think about *The Sisters*. Who are the characters? Choose ✔ or ✘.

回想一下故事，里面都有谁？判断正误。

1. Kay and Ella. ✔ ✘
2. Kay, Fran, and Ella. ✔ ✘
3. Kay, Fran, and Patty. ✔ ✘

C Listen to *The Sisters* again. Choose the correct answer.

再听一听故事，选择正确的答案。

1. What color is the house?
   - [x] a. Blue.
   - [ ] b. White.
   - [ ] c. Green.
2. What can Kay do?
   - [ ] a. Sing.
   - [ ] b. Jump.
   - [ ] c. Dance.
3. Who has red hair?
   - [ ] a. The tall sister.
   - [ ] b. The short sister.
   - [ ] c. The baby.
4. What can the baby do?
   - [ ] a. Jump.
   - [ ] b. Skip.
   - [ ] c. Stamp.

D Listen and write the word. Then choose the correct picture.

听一听，写出正确的单词，并选择相应的图片。

1. legs

☑ a

☐ b

2. ____________

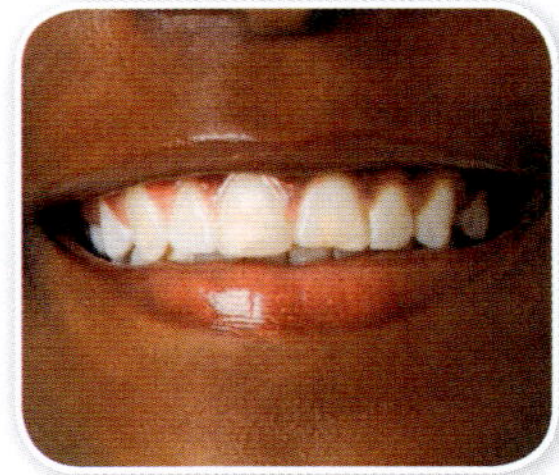
☐ a

☐ b

3. ____________

☐ a

☐ b

4. ____________

☐ a

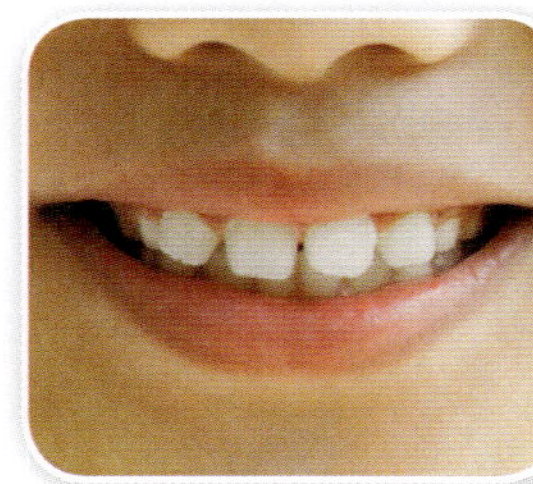
☐ b

E Complete the sentences. 选一选，填一填（每个选项限用一次）。

teeth	~~body~~	head	legs

1. An elephant has a big body.
2. The baby has two new ____________.
3. A mouse has short ____________.
4. Tom has a hat on his ____________.

F Unscramble and write. 理一理，写出正确的单词。

1. e a d h

head

2. h t e t e

____

3. s l g e

____

4. o d y b

____

WORKBOOK
UNIT
12

Listen

LISTENING GOAL: Listen for the Speaker

听力训练目标：明确讲话者是谁

Remember!
Listen for **names**. They tell who the **speaker** is.
注意听名字，名字能告诉我们是谁在说话。

A Listen to the interview *The Acrobat*. Then put the pictures in order.

听一听这段采访录音，给图片排序。

A

☐

B

1

C
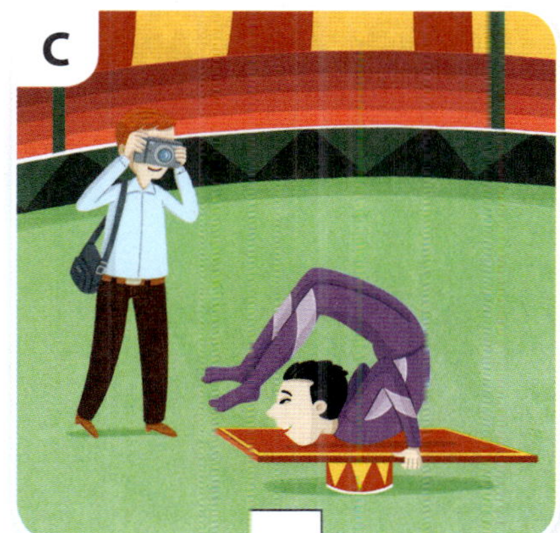
☐

B Think about *The Acrobat*. Who are the speakers? Choose ✔ or ✘.

回想一下采访内容，里面的讲话者都有谁？判断正误。

1. Henri. ✔ ✘
2. Ruby. ✔ ✘
3. Pierre. ✔ ✘

C Listen to *The Acrobat* again. Choose Yes or No.

再听一听录音，判断正误。

1. Pierre can walk on his hands. (Yes) No
2. He can make a T with his body. Yes No
3. He can touch his eyes with his feet. Yes No
4. He can touch his nose with his knees. Yes No
5. Henri wants to draw a picture. Yes No
6. Henri is an acrobat. Yes No

D Listen. Then read and choose the correct answer.

听一听，读一读，并选择正确的答案。

1. What can she touch?

a. 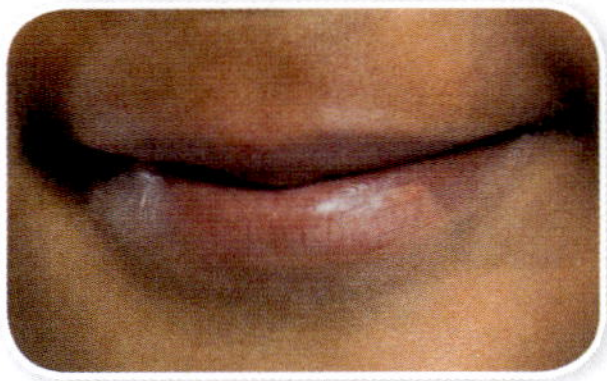

(b.) 

c. 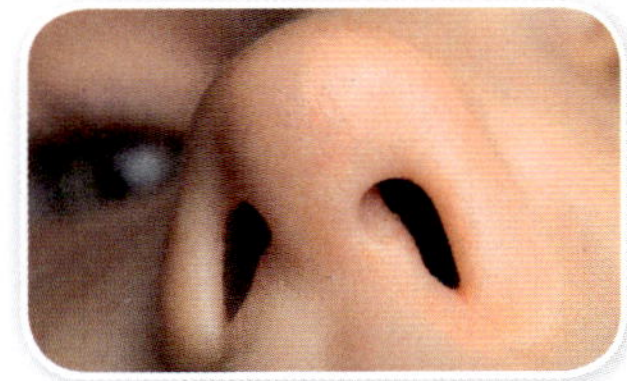

2. What is it?

a. 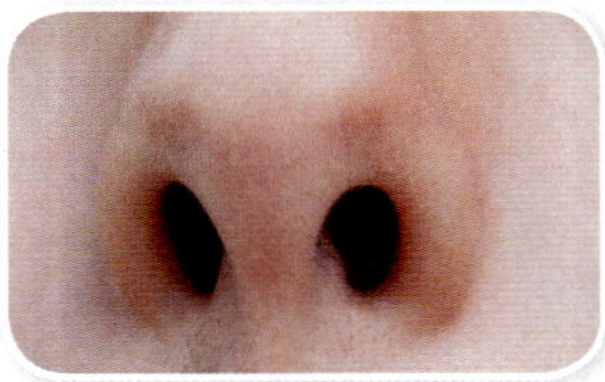

b. 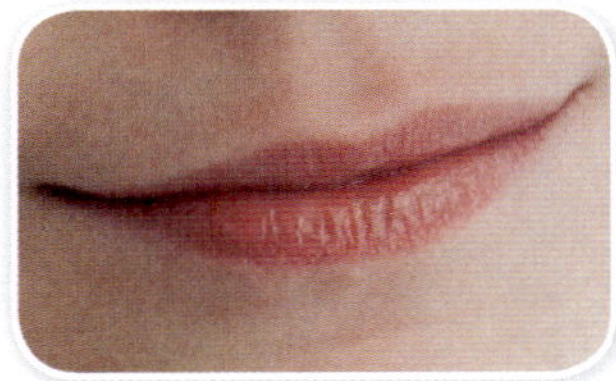

c. 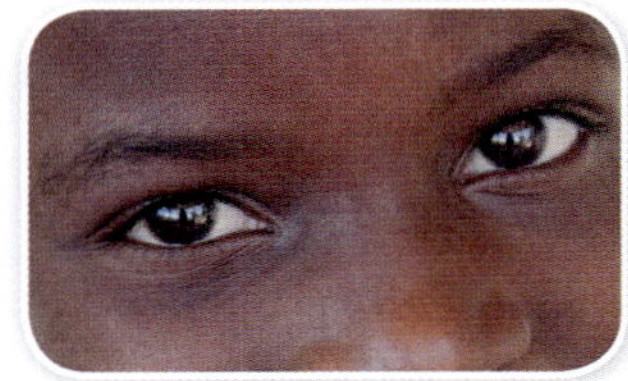

3. What is pretty?

a. 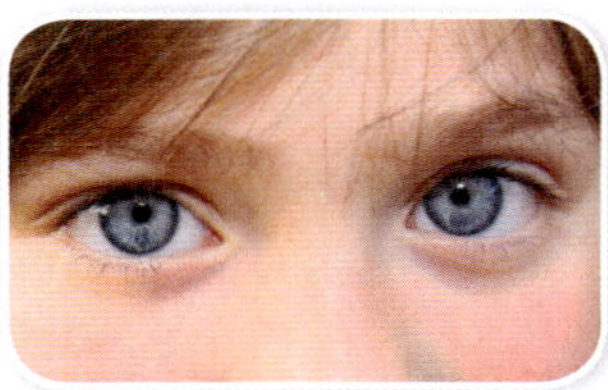

b. 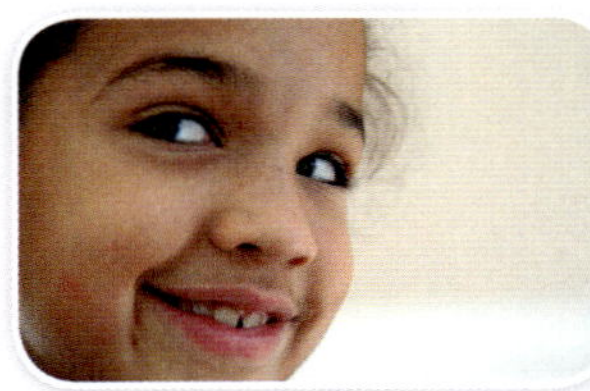

c. 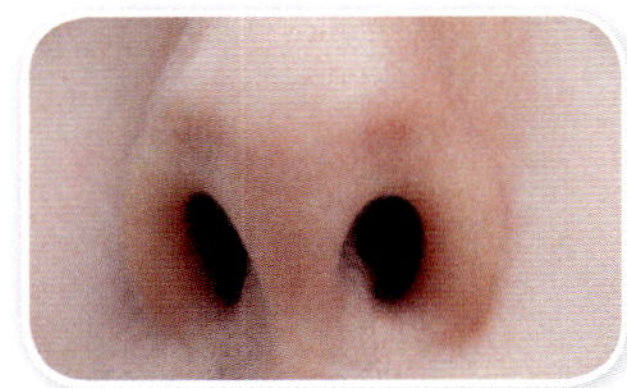

E Complete the sentences. 根据首字母提示，用本单元的重点词汇补全句子。

1. He has a round ______face______.
2. The tiger has a big m______________.
3. Sunita has brown e______________.
4. Ouch! I hurt my n______________.

Speak

Remember!
Use *I'm* and *It's* in your descriptions.
描述时可以使用I'm 和It's。

Circle *I'm* and *It's*. Then think of your own sentences with *I'm* and *It's*. Tell your partner.

圈出句子中的 I'm 和 It's，然后用它们造几个句子，和小伙伴说一说。

I can play tennis. It's fun.

I play tag. I run and run. I'm hot.

Picture Dictionary

Write the key words.
写出重点词汇。

Unit 1

Unit 2

Unit 3

Unit 4

Unit 5

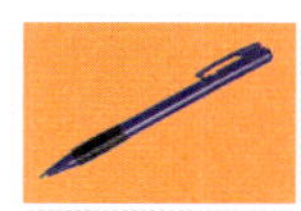

Unit 6

Unit 7

Unit 9

Unit 11

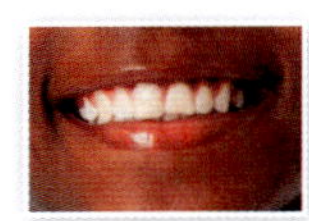

Unit 8

Unit 10

Unit 12

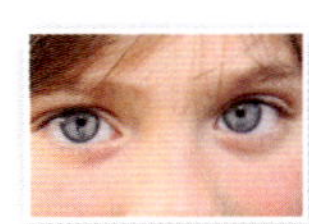

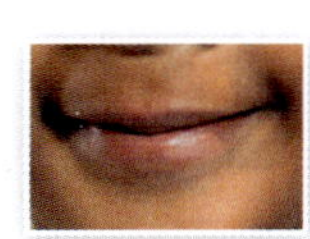

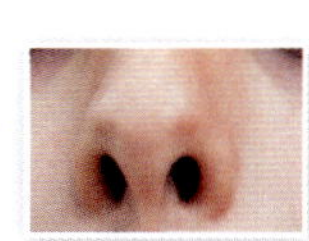

Answer Key

pp6–7

A
1. Answers will vary.
2. Answers will vary.

B
1. It helps goats and cows.
2. Answers will vary.

p8

B
Students color the monkey brown.
Students color the sheep white.
Students color the cow black.
Students color the duck green.

C
1. sheep
2. cow
3. monkey
4. duck

p9

A
1. Yes
2. No
3. Yes

B
A
a. 3
b. 1
c. 2

pp10–11

A
a

B
1. sheep
2. water
3. duck
4. jumps
5. Tom

C
1. sheep, d
2. monkey, c
3. cow, b
4. duck, a

D
1. It isn't
2. It's
3. It's
4. It isn't
5. It's

E
1. It isn't, It's
2. It's
3. It's
4. It isn't, It's

p12

B
1. crocodile
2. mouse
3. giraffe
4. elephant

C
1. mouse
2. crocodile
3. giraffe
4. elephant

p13

A
1. ✗
2. ✓
3. ✓

B
A
1. ✓
2. ✗
3. ✓

pp14–15

A
1. Yes
2. No

B
1. b
2. b
3. a

C
1. b, giraffe
2. a, elephant
3. b, crocodile
4. a, mouse

D
1. in the water
2. on the grass
3. under the tree
4. by the bus

E
1. in
2. on
3. under
4. by

pp16–17

A
B

B
1. ✗
2. ✓
3. ✗
4. ✗

C
1. ✗
2. ✗
3. ✓
4. ✗

D
1. b
2. a
3. a
4. b
5. c

E
(1) elephant
(2) duck
(3) mouse
(4) monkey

pp18–19

A
Underline: My, I, I, I

B
1. Jin-Goo Kim
2. 8
3. Seoul
4. cats

C
Answers will vary.

D
Answers will vary.

pp20–21

A
1. Answers will vary.
2. Answers will vary.

B
1. The people throw colors.
2. Answers will vary.

p22

B
Students color the swim ring (circle) orange.
Students color the blanket (square) purple.
Students color the teddy bear pink.
Students color the book brown.

C
1. circle
2. brown
3. white
4. square

p23

A
1. three
2. one
3. five

B
B

a. 1
b. 3
c. 2

pp24–25

A
a

B
1. Hannah
2. two
3. white
4. brown
5. three

C
1. square, b
2. white, a
3. brown, d
4. circle, c

D
1. brown, circle
2. white, square

E
1. this
2. this
3. Is, brown
4. this, white

p26

B
1. a girl's red cap
2. the other girl's blue cap
3. a girl's yellow paint
4. the other girl's green paint

C
1. green
2. red
3. blue
4. yellow

p27

A
1. ✓
2. ✗
3. ✓

B
A
1. ✓
2. ✓
3. ✗

pp28–29

A
1. No
2. Yes

B
1. a
2. b
3. a

C
1. b, green
2. a, yellow
3. a, blue
4. b, red

D
1. a green guitar
2. a red skateboard
3. a blue balloon
4. a yellow car

E
1. has
2. has
3. don't have, have
4. don't have, have

pp30–31

A
B

B
1. ✗
2. ✓
3. ✓
4. ✗

C
1. ✓
2. ✓
3. ✗
4. ✗

D
1. b
2. c
3. a
4. b
5. b

E
(1) circles
(2) yellow
(3) red
(4) Green

pp32–33

A
Tree: big, green, brown
Sun: circle, yellow

B
1. big
2. green
3. brown
4. circle
5. yellow

C
Answers will vary.

D
Answers will vary.

pp34–35

A
1. Answers will vary.
2. Answers will vary.

B
1. It can talk. It can dance. It knows how you feel. It can be a good friend.
2. Answers will vary.

p36

B
Students color the notebook yellow.
Students color the car blue.
Students color the pen red.
Students color the eraser green.

C
1. notebook
2. draw
3. eraser
4. pen

p37

A
1. hi
2. see you later
3. hello

B
B
a. 2
b. 3
c. 1

pp38–39

A
b

B
1. notebook
2. zoo
3. lion
4. an eraser
5. doesn't like

C
1. pen, b
2. eraser, c
3. draw, a
4. notebook, d

D
1. notebook
2. pen
3. pencil
4. eraser

E
1. is
2. my
3. is
4. This

p40

B
1. class
2. backpack
3. ruler
4. paper

C
1. paper
2. class
3. ruler
4. backpack

p41

A
1. pencil
2. book
3. table

B
B
1. ✓
2. ✗
3. ✓

pp42–43

A
1. No

2. Yes

B

1. b
2. a
3. a

C

1. b, backpack
2. a, ruler
3. a, class
4. b, paper

D

1. What's
2. Is it
3. Is it
4. Is it

E

1. It
2. Is
3. isn't
4. it, it

pp44–45

A

C

B

1. ✗
2. ✓
3. ✗
4. ✓

C

1. ✓
2. ✗
3. ✗
4. ✓

D

1. b
2. c
3. c
4. a
5. a

E

(1) backpack
(2) paper
(3) pen
(4) eraser

pp46–47

A

Underline: Hello, Hi, See you later, Goodbye

B

1. hello
2. hi
3. see you later
4. goodbye

C

Answers will vary.

D

Answers will vary.

pp48–49

A

1. Answers will vary.
2. Answers will vary.

B

1. They eat fast. They eat a lot.
2. Answers will vary.

p50

B

Students color the parents' picture blue.
Students color the children's picture green.
Students color the girl's picture red.
Students color the boy's picture yellow.

C

1. girl
2. children
3. parents
4. boy

p51

A

1. who
2. where
3. what

B

A

1. ✓
2. ✗
3. ✗

pp52–53

A

b

B

1. Matt's
2. beach
3. Jason
4. girl
5. likes

C

1. parents, b
2. children, d
3. boy, a
4. girl, c

D

1. Who
2. Where
3. Who
4. What

E

1. Who are they?
2. Where/What is this?
3. Who are the children?
4. What is this?

p54

B

1. family
2. grandparents
3. uncle
4. cousin

C

1. grandparents
2. family
3. uncle
4. cousin

p55

A

1. ✓
2. ✗
3. ✓

B

A

a. 1
b. 3
c. 2

pp56–57

A

1. Yes
2. No

B

1. a
2. a
3. b

C

1. b, grandparents
2. a, uncle
3. b, family
4. a, cousin

D

1. big
2. fun
3. tall
4. pretty

E

1. It's
2. It's
3. He's
4. She's

pp58–59

A

B

B

1. ✓
2. ✓
3. ✗
4. ✓

C

1. ✗
2. ✗
3. ✓
4. ✓

D

1. b
2. a
3. c
4. a
5. c

E

(1) boys
(2) cousin
(3) children
(4) parents

pp60–61

A

Underline: Who, Where, How

B

1. Who is this?
2. Where does he live?
3. How old is he?

C

Answers will vary.

D
Answers will vary.

pp62–63

A
1. Answers will vary.
2. Answers will vary.

B
1. It's long and fast.
2. Answers will vary.

p64

B
Students color the bike brown.
Students color the teddy bear pink.
Students color the boat orange.
Students color the scooter blue.

C
1. boat
2. scooter
3. teddy bear
4. bike

p65

A
1. ball
2. train
3. apples

B
B
a. 2
b. 1
c. 3

pp66–67

A
a

B
1. balloon
2. big
3. little
4. fast
5. gets

C
1. boat, c
2. bike, a
3. teddy bear, d
4. scooter, b

D
1. balloon
2. bike
3. boat
4. scooter

E
1. likes
2. likes
3. like
4. likes

p68

B
1. carrots
2. peach
3. tomato
4. mango

C
1. carrots
2. tomato
3. mango
4. peach

p69

A
1. ✓
2. ✗
3. ✓

B
A
1. ✗
2. ✓
3. ✗

pp70–71

A
b

B
1. b
2. a
3. b

C
1. a, tomato
2. b, mango
3. a, peach
4. b, carrots

D
1. carrots
2. tomatoes
3. salad
4. mangoes

E
1. don't like
2. don't like
3. doesn't like
4. doesn't like

pp72–73

A
C

B
1. ✗
2. ✓
3. ✓
4. ✓

C
1. ✓
2. ✗
3. ✓
4. ✗

D
1. a
2. a
3. b
4. b
5. a

E
(1) scooter
(2) bikes
(3) carrots
(4) peaches

pp74–75

A
Underline: but, and, but

B
1. video games
2. mangoes
3. bananas
4. books
5. puppets
6. mangoes
7. bananas

C
Answers will vary.

D
Answers will vary.

pp76–77

A
1. Answers will vary.
2. Answers will vary.

B
1. She uses her hands and feet.
2. Answers will vary.

p78

B
Students color the kangaroo's head brown.
Students color the kangaroo's legs black.
Students color the donkey's body gray.
Students color the kangaroo's teeth white.

C
1. legs
2. body
3. teeth
4. head

p79

A
1. Harry
2. John
3. June

B
B
a. 2
b. 3
c. 1

pp80–81

A
b

B
1. head
2. legs
3. little
4. Max
5. big

C
1. legs, d
2. teeth, c
3. head, a
4. body, b

D
1. big
2. big
3. long
4. big

E
1. big
2. big
3. long
4. big

p82

B
1. long nose
2. Jo's eyes
3. happy face
4. Jo's mouth

C
1. face
2. eyes
3. nose
4. mouth

p83

A
1. ✓
2. ✓
3. ✗

B
A
1. ✗
2. ✓
3. ✓

pp84–85

A
1. Yes
2. No

B
1. b
2. b
3. a

C
1. a, face
2. b, nose
3. a, eyes
4. b, mouth

D
1. a mouth
2. a nose
3. eyes

E
1. She can make a cake.
2. She can make a mouth.
3. She can make a nose.
4. She can make eyes.

pp86–87

A
A

B
1. ✓
2. ✗
3. ✓
4. ✓

C
1. Shoma
2. Lucy
3. Shoma
4. Maya

D
1. c
2. a
3. a
4. c
5. b

E
(1) nose
(2) teeth
(3) eyes
(4) legs

pp88–89

A
Underline: It's, It's I'm

B
1. soccer
2. in the park
3. happy

C
Answers will vary.

D
Answers will vary.

Workbook Answer Key

pp91–92

A
1. ✗
2. ✓

B
1. ✓
2. ✗
3. ✓

C
1. b
2. c
3. a
4. b

D
1. duck, b
2. monkey, a
3. sheep, a
4. cow, b

E
1. cow
2. monkey
3. duck
4. sheep

F
1. duck
2. sheep
3. monkey
4. cow

pp93–94

A
2, 3, 1

B
1. ✗
2. ✓
3. ✗

C
1. No
2. No
3. Yes
4. No
5. Yes
6. Yes

D
1. b
2. a
3. a

E
1. elephant
2. mouse
3. giraffe
4. crocodile

Speak
Circle: I, my, I, my

pp95–96

A
1. ✓
2. ✗

B
1. ✓
2. ✓
3. ✗

C
1. a

2. b
3. c
4. b

D
1. white, a
2. circle, b
3. brown, b
4. square, a

E
1. white
2. circle
3. brown
4. square

F
1. brown
2. white
3. circle
4. square

pp97–98

A
1, 3, 2

B
1. ✗
2. ✗
3. ✓

C
1. No
2. Yes
3. No
4. No
5. Yes
6. No

D
1. c
2. a
3. b

E
1. blue
2. yellow
3. green
4. red

Speak
Circle: green, little, new

pp99–100

A
1. ✗
2. ✓

B
1. ✗
2. ✓
3. ✗

C
1. a
2. b
3. c
4. a

D
1. notebook, a
2. draw, b
3. eraser, a
4. pen, b

E
1. notebook
2. draw
3. pen
4. eraser

F
1. eraser
2. pen
3. notebook
4. draw

pp101–102

A
3, 1, 2

B
1. ✗
2. ✓
3. ✓

C
1. Yes
2. No
3. No
4. Yes
5. Yes
6. No

D
1. a
2. a
3. c

E
1. backpack
2. ruler
3. class
4. paper

Speak
Circle: Hi, See you later

Answers will vary.

pp103–104

A
1. ✓
2. ✗

B
1. ✓
2. ✗
3. ✓

C
1. c
2. b
3. a
4. c

D
1. children, b
2. girl, b
3. boy, a
4. parents, a

E
1. parents
2. boy
3. children
4. girl

F
1. boy
2. parents
3. children
4. girl

pp105–106

A
1, 3, 2

B
1. ✓
2. ✗
3. ✗

C
1. No
2. Yes
3. Yes
4. No
5. No
6. Yes

D
1. c
2. b
3. b

E
1. cousin
2. uncle
3. family
4. grandparents

Speak
Circle: Who, Where
Answers will vary.

pp107–108

A
1. ✗
2. ✓

B
1. ✗
2. ✗
3. ✓

C
1. c
2. a
3. b
4. c

D
1. bike, a
2. boat, b
3. scooter, b
4. teddy bear, a

E
1. teddy bear
2. boat
3. scooter
4. bike

F
1. scooter
2. bike
3. teddy bear
4. boat

pp109–110

A
1, 3, 2

B
1. ✓
2. ✗
3. ✓

C
1. ✓
2. ✗
3. ✗
4. ✓
5. ✓

6. ✗

D

1. a
2. b
3. a

E

1. tomato
2. mango
3. peach
4. carrots

Speak

Circle: and, but
Answers will vary.

pp111–112

A

1. ✓
2. ✗

B

1. ✗
2. ✓
3. ✗

C

1. a
2. b
3. b
4. c

D

1. legs, a
2. head, b
3. body, b
4. teeth, b

E

1. body
2. teeth
3. legs
4. head

F

1. head
2. teeth
3. legs
4. body

pp113–114

A

2, 1, 3

B

1. ✓
2. ✗
3. ✓

C

1. Yes
2. Yes
3. Yes
4. No
5. No
6. No

D

1. b
2. a
3. a

E

1. face
2. mouth
3. eyes
4. nose

Speak

Circle: It's, I'm
Answers will vary.

Audio Script

p7

B

A Friendly Animal

The llama helps goats and cows! It kicks and runs.

p8

A

cow, duck, monkey, sheep

B

The monkey is brown.
The sheep is white.
The cow is black.
The duck is green.

C

1. sheep
2. cow
3. monkey
4. duck

p9

A

1. *Mr. Frog*
   Mr. Frog likes rain. He jumps and jumps. Mr. Frog sees a puddle. "1, 2, 3, jump! I like rain!"
2. *The Bananas*
   Monkey is hungry. She wants bananas. Monkey climbs a big tree. She finds three bananas!
3. *Bird and the Books*
   Bird likes to read. Bird reads at home. He has books about planes. He has books about the weather.

B

Three Friends

"I like this farm," says Dan.
"Look! There's a cow!"
"It isn't a cow," says Jane.
"It's a sheep."
They go to the water.
"Look! It's a duck," says Dan.
They go to a tree.
What do they see?
"It's a monkey!" says Jane.
The monkey jumps.
"It isn't a monkey!" says Dan.
"It's Tom!"

p10

B

See script of *Three Friends*.

C

1. They see a sheep.
2. The monkey sees the boy.
3. The cow is at the farm.
4. They point to the duck.

p11

D

See script of *Three Friends*.

p12

A

crocodile, elephant, giraffe, mouse

B

1. The crocodile is by the rock.
2. The mouse is by the tree.
3. The giraffe is by the tree.
4. The elephant is very big.

C

1. The mouse eats a lot.
2. The crocodile can run.
3. The giraffe can kick.
4. The elephant likes bananas.

p13

A

1. A pet is an animal. We have pets at home. A cat can be a pet.
2. What do rabbits eat? They eat grass! They have long teeth. They can eat a lot of grass!
3. Bees get food from flowers. They like yellow flowers. They like blue and purple flowers, too.

B

Animal Fun

The boys and girls go on a safari. They ride on a bus. They can see many animals. The crocodile is in the water. The elephant is on the grass. The giraffe is under the tree. There's a mouse! The mouse is by the bus! The boys and girls are happy. A safari is fun.

p14

B

See script of *Animal Fun*.

C

1. The giraffe has knees.
2. The elephant is very big.
3. The crocodile can swim.
4. The mouse has big ears.

p15

D

See script of *Animal Fun*.

p16

A

A Night at the Zoo

Sarah and Jim are at the zoo.
It is night.
Sarah! I see something!
What is it, Jim?
I don't know.
It's an elephant!
It isn't an elephant. It's little.
It's a duck.
It isn't a duck. It has a long tail.
It's a mouse!
No! It's a monkey! And it's under an umbrella!

p17

D

See script of *A Night at the Zoo*.

E

See script of *A Night at the Zoo*.

p18

A

Hello! My name is Jin-Goo Kim.
I am 8 years old.
I live in Seoul. It is a city in South Korea.
I like cats.

p21

B

A Fun Run

This is a fun run. There are many people. They throw a lot of colors. The people are happy.

p22

A

brown, circle, square, white

B

The circle is orange.
The square is purple.
The teddy bear is pink.
The book is brown.

C

1. circle
2. brown
3. white
4. square

p23

A

1. Susan has some dolls. How many? Count the dolls. 1, 2, 3.
2. Look, Gina. Is this a black

train? Yes, it is.
3. How many pencils does Max have? Five. Five pencils.

B
Cookie Count
Hi, Oscar! I have cookies.
Hi, Hannah! Look at this cookie. Is this a square?
No, it isn't. It's a circle. It's a brown circle.
Five brown circles. And this cookie? Is this a square?
Yes, it is. It's a white square.
Three white squares. I eat one. Now you have seven cookies!
Oscar!

p24

B
See script of *Cookie Count*.

C
1. This is a square.
2. The teapot is white.
3. It's a brown nest.
4. It's a circle.

p25

D
See script of *Cookie Count*.

p26

A
blue, green, red, yellow

B
1. There is a girl with a red cap.
2. There is a girl with a blue cap.
3. She has yellow paint.
4. She has green paint.

C
1. The pencil is green.
2. He has a red vest.
3. She is in the blue car.
4. I have a yellow yo-yo.

p27

A
1. Look at the car! What color is it?
   It's red.
2. Where is the ball?
   It's in the box. It's a green ball.
3. I have a bag. It's an orange bag. It's pretty.

B
Fred the Clown
Fred is a clown. He has a green guitar. He has a red skateboard. He has a blue balloon. But where is Fred's car?
"I don't have my yellow car!" says Fred.
There's Joe. Joe is in a yellow car. It's Fred's car!
"Joe!" says Fred. "You have my car!"
"Oh!" says Joe. "I'm sorry!"

p28

B
See script of *Fred the Clown*.

C
1. Fred has a green guitar.
2. Fred has a yellow car.
3. Fred has a blue balloon.
4. Fred has a red skateboard.

p29

D
See script of *Fred the Clown*.

p30

A
Traffic Light
I draw three circles.
One, two, three.
I see circles.
Red, yellow, green.
I have red.
Red says "stop!"
I have yellow.
Yellow says "slow."
I have green.
Green says "go!"
One black box. I have black.
This is a traffic light.
Go, crayons, go!
Vrooom!

p31

D
See script of *Traffic Light*.

E
See script of *Traffic Light*.

p32

A
The Park
This is a tree. It's big.
It's green and brown.
This is the sun. It's a circle.
It's yellow.

p35

B
A Robot at School
Can robots help at school?
This robot can talk. It can dance. It knows how you feel. It can be a good friend.

p36

A
draw, eraser, notebook, pen

B
The notebook is yellow.
Alice draws a blue car.
She has a red pen.
The eraser is green.

C
1. notebook
2. draw
3. eraser
4. pen

p37

A
1. Hi, Ella! This is my friend, Erin.
2. Thank you for the pencil, Kelly. See you later!
3. Hello, Kayo. Do you have your book?

B
The Special Notebook
Hi, Paul!
Hi, Mei! This is my special notebook. I have a pen and a pencil. I can draw a picture, and we can go there!
Draw a zoo! Whoa!
It's a lion! Run!
Use your eraser! Make the lion go away!
OK! We're home!
I don't like that notebook.
See you later.
OK. Goodbye.

p38

B
See script of *The Special Notebook*.

C
1. This is my pen.
2. The eraser is little.
3. I draw at the table.
4. It's my notebook.

p39

D
See script of *The Special Notebook*.

p40

A
backpack, class, paper, ruler

B
1. There are three boys and three girls in my class.
2. This girl has a new back-pack.
3. She has a ruler.
4. The paper is green.

C
1. The paper is in the cup-board.
2. This is my class.
3. It's a ruler.
4. I have a big backpack.

p41

A
1. This is a pencil. The pencil is long.
2. The book is fun. The book has many pictures.
3. The table is big. There is a flower on the table.

B
The Box
What's in the box?

It's a present for you!
A present!
Yes, a present!
Is it a ruler?
No, it isn't.
Is it paper?
No, it isn't.
What is the present? Is it a backpack?
Yes, it is! It's a backpack!
Thank you, Mom! I can take the backpack to class!

p42

B
See script of *The Box*.

C
1. Is it a backpack?
2. Is it a ruler?
3. Can I take it to class?
4. Is it paper?

p43

D
See script of *The Box*.

p44

A
Mouse and Frog
"Hello, Mouse!" says Frog.
"Hello, Frog! Look in my backpack! I have a pen and paper. And this is my eraser."
Mouse is happy. He jumps.
The pen and eraser jump, too.
"Where are my pen and eraser?"
"This is your pen. This is your eraser!" says Frog.
"Thank you!"
"See you later!" says Frog.

p45

D
See script of *Mouse and Frog*.

E
See script of *Mouse and Frog*.

p46

A
Hello, Mark!
Hi, Trang!
Look! I have a doll in my backpack!
It's a nice doll!
Thank you. See you later!
Goodbye, Trang!

p49

B
Watermelon Fun
This is a game. The girl and her brother eat watermelon. They eat very fast. They eat a lot of watermelon!

p50

A
parents, boy, girl, children

B
The parents' picture is blue.
The children's picture is green.
The girl's picture is red.
The boy's picture is yellow.

C
1. girl
2. children
3. parents
4. boy

p51

A
1. Who is he?
   He's my father. He's at my house.
2. Where is this?
   This is the park. There are a lot of trees.
3. What is this?
   It's a crayon. It's orange.

B
My Family
Meg looks at Matt's picture.
"Who are they?" asks Meg.
"They are my parents," says Matt.
"Where is this?"
"This is the beach."
"Who are the children?" asks Meg.
"This is Jason," says Matt.
"He's a boy. This is Jessie. She's a girl. And this is me!"
"What is this?"
"It's fish," says Matt. "We like fish!"

p52

B
See script of *My Family*.

C
1. My parents are at the beach.
2. I can see the children.
3. The boy has a cup.
4. The girl has a cup, too.

p53

D
See script of *My Family*.

p54

A
grandparents, uncle, cousin, family

B
1. This is my family.
2. My grandparents like the food.
3. My uncle has a watch.
4. My cousin is happy.

C
1. My grandparents are at home.
2. The teacher talks to my family.
3. My uncle likes pizza.
4. My cousin is in my class.

p55

A
1. How many cousins do you have?
   I have three cousins.
2. Where is your grandmother?
   My grandmother is in the store.
3. What is this?
   It's a plane. It's red and blue.

B
My Summer
Hello, class. See my picture?
This is my summer.
Where is this?
This is my grandparents' house. It's big.
What is this?
It's a game. I play with my family. It's fun!
Who is this?
He's my uncle. He's my mom's brother. We ride bicycles!
He's tall. Is this your cousin?
Yes. My uncle is her dad.
She's pretty.

p56

B
See script of *My Summer*.

C
1. These are my grandparents.
2. My uncle lives in China.
3. This is my family.
4. He's my cousin.

p57

D
See script of *My Summer*.

p58

A
Apple Farm
Three boys are at an apple farm.
Where is John?
Who is John?
He's my cousin.
There are some children. I see a boy. Is he tall?
Yes, he is. He has a blue cap.
He's with your parents! He's under the tree.
John! Do you have apples?
Yes, I have 10 apples!

p59

D
See script of *Apple Farm*.

E
See script of *Apple Farm*.

p60

A
Who is this?
This is my cousin.
Where does he live?

He lives in Canada.
How old is he?
He's 11 years old.

p63

B
A Roller Coaster
This is a roller coaster. It's long. It's fast! It goes up and down! Some children like roller coasters, and some children don't!

p64

A
bike, boat, scooter, teddy bear

B
The bike is brown.
The teddy bear is pink.
The boat is orange.
The scooter is blue.

C
1. boat
2. scooter
3. teddy bear
4. bike

p65

A
1. I like my ball. I can throw it. It's fun.
2. I like to ride on the train. I can see many people and places.
3. I like the apples. I can get some for my mom.

B
Teddy Bear and Bird
Teddy Bear likes his new balloon. He rides a bike with his balloon. He likes the bike. It's big. Bird rides a scooter. She likes the scooter. It's little. They see a boat. They go for a ride.
"I like this boat!" says Teddy Bear. "It's fast!" The balloon flies away!
Bird flies up! She gets the balloon!

p66

B
See script of *Teddy Bear and Bird.*

C
1. I see a blue boat.
2. He rides a bike.
3. Is this your teddy bear?
4. She has a new scooter.

p67

D
See script of *Teddy Bear and Bird.*

p68

A
carrots, mango, peach, tomato

B
1. She wants some carrots.
2. She likes the peach.
3. The man has a tomato.
4. He has a mango.

C
1. The carrots are on the table.
2. He eats the tomato.
3. I don't have a mango.
4. Where is the peach?

p69

A
1. I don't want milk.
2. I don't like fish.
3. I don't like tomatoes.

B
Pete and Mia
Pete and Mia are hungry. Pete likes carrots. He likes tomatoes, too. He makes a salad.
"Yuck. I don't like carrots, and I don't like tomatoes," says Mia. She doesn't like the salad. Mia doesn't like mangoes. She likes peaches. She makes a cake. "I like this cake."
Now Pete and Mia are happy.

p70

B
See script of *Pete and Mia*.

C
1. We can make a tomato salad.
2. Do you have mango smoothies?
3. I don't like this peach.
4. I don't like to eat carrots.

p71

D
See script of *Pete and Mia*.

p72

A
What Do You Like?
Jake and Ben play outdoors.
"I like my scooter. It's fast!" says Jake.
But Ben doesn't like scooters. They're little. Ben likes bikes!
Jake and Ben are hungry.
"I like carrots," says Jake.
But Ben doesn't like carrots. He likes peaches.
"Boys!" says Ben's mom. "Do you want chicken?"
They like chicken! They go!

p73

D
See script of *What Do You Like?*.

E
See script of *What Do You Like?*.

p74

A
I like video games, but I don't like books. What do you like?
I like puppets. Do you like fruit?
Yes, I like mangoes and bananas.
I like mangoes, but I don't like bananas.

p77

B
Up, Up, Up!
This is a big wall. It's a rock wall. I go up the wall. I use my hands and feet.

p78

A
body, head, legs, teeth

B
The kangaroo has a brown head.
The kangaroo's legs are black.
The donkey's body is gray.
The kangaroo has white teeth

C
1. legs
2. body
3. teeth
4. head

p79

A
1. Harry the lion has big ears. He can hear the birds.
2. I can see two hands. They are John's hands.
3. The new girl is June. She's tall, and she can run fast.

B
Tim Tiger and Friends
Tim Tiger, Max Mouse, and Heidi Hen are friends
Tim has a big head. He has a big body. He has long legs. Max has a triangle. It's little. Tim jumps. Oh, no! He's in the triangle! He can't get out! Max pulls Tim. Heidi pulls Max. Tim comes out! Tim smiles. He has big teeth.

p80

B
See script of *Tim Tiger and Friends.*

C
1. We have two legs.

2. I brush my teeth.
3. I can touch my head.
4. This is my body.

p81

D

See script of *Tim Tiger and Friends*.

p82

A

eyes, face, mouth, nose

B

1. Mo has a long nose.
2. Jo has round eyes.
3. Mo has a happy face.
4. Jo has a big mouth.

C

1. My face is little and round.
2. I can touch my eyes.
3. I have a long nose.
4. This is my mouth.

p83

A

1. Hello. My name is Sally. My presentation is about birds. They have good eyes.
2. Hi, Cora. This is my friend, Kenny.
   Hello, Kenny.
   Hi, Cora!
3. Hello, Grace. What do you have?
   Hi, Ryota. It's pizza.
   Can I have some?

B

Funny Face

Anna and Mike make a cake.
I have a banana. I can make a mouth. What can you do?
I have cherries, Anna. I can make eyes.
I have an apple. I can make a nose. Is that a face?
Yes! The cake has a face!
That's funny, Mike!
Let's take the cake to Jacob!

p84

B

See script of *Funny Face*.

C

1. The face is round.
2. The nose is big.
3. These are my eyes.
4. I have a little mouth.

p85

D

See script of *Funny Face*.

p86

A

What Is It?

Lucy, Shoma, and Maya are at the zoo.
"I see something!" says Shoma.
"What is it?" asks Lucy.
"I don't know."
"It has a big nose!" says Maya.
"It has little teeth!" says Shoma.
"It has round eyes!" says Lucy.
"It has short legs!" says Maya.
It's a baby lion!
The lion jumps.

C

See script of *What Is It?*.

p87

D

See script of *What Is It?*.

E

See script of *What Is It?*.

p88

A

My Favorite Activity

I like soccer. It's fun.
I play in the park. It's big.
I'm happy.

p91

A

A Friend for Duck

Duck wants a friend. Cow helps Duck. They are at the farm.
"I see a duck!" says Duck.
"It isn't a duck," says Cow.
"It's a sheep."
"There's a duck!"
"No," says Cow. "It's a goat."
"I see a duck!"
"Yes!" says Cow.
"There are ten little ducks!" says Duck. "Now I have many friends!"

C

See script of *A Friend for Duck*.

p92

D

1. duck
2. monkey
3. sheep
4. cow

p93

A

City Zoo

Amy and Don are at City Zoo. It is a lot of fun!
Don, there are three crocodiles. They're in the water.
Yes, they're long! Where is the elephant?
It's under the tree. It's big!
I'm hungry.
I have an apple.
Thank you. Oh! A bee! It's on the apple!

C

See script of *City Zoo*.

p94

D

1. The girl sees a mouse.
2. There is a giraffe at the zoo.
3. The crocodile is old.

p95

A

A Robot

Min-Jun has paper. He and Sue make a robot.
Is this a brown square?
Yes, it is. There are two brown squares.
Is this a purple rectangle?
Yes, it is. There are four purple rectangles.
Look at this heart. It's pink!
Yes, it's a pink heart. It's for the robot.
The robot likes us!

C

See script of *A Robot*.

p96

D

1. white
2. circle
3. brown
4. square

p97

A

Ice Cream Juice

It's hot today. Kate has ice cream. She has three blue scoops. She has two green scoops. She has one red scoop. Kate is hungry. Where is Yuki? He's at school. Yuki comes in. He looks at the ice cream. "Oh! We don't have ice cream! We have ice cream juice!" says Yuki.

C

See script of *Ice Cream Juice*.

p98

D

1. He has a blue umbrella.
2. She has a red jump rope.
3. I have a green kite.

p99

A

Bob's Day

It's a nice day. Bob wants to play, but he has school.
"Hi, Bob!" says Mom.
"Hi, Mom," says Bob. "Where is my pen?"
"It's on the table."
"Where is my notebook?"
"Why?"
"It's for school," says Bob.
"School?" says Mom. "Today is Sunday!"
"Sunday?" says Bob. "I can play! See you later, Mom!"

C

See script of *Bob's Day*.

p100

D

1. notebook
2. draw
3. eraser
4. pen

p101

A

My Picture

Hello, class! This is my picture. There are many colors.

I have some paper. It isn't paint. And these are my scissors. I use paper and scissors. See, I can make a circle. I can make many shapes!

Now you can make pictures, too. Can you take out your paper and scissors?

C

See script of *My Picture*.

p102

D

1. The teacher has a ruler.
2. The backpack is on the table.
3. The paper is in the bag.

p103

A

The Snow Family

Rina and Hugo play in the snow.

"What is this?" asks Rina.

"It's my snowman. He's a boy. He's Sam."

"Who are they?"

"They're Sam's parents."

A little girl plays. She kicks Sam!

Hugo and Rina look.

Where is Sam?

He's by the gate! But he isn't a snowman. He's a snowball!

C

See script of *The Snow Family*.

p104

D

1. children
2. girl
3. boy
4. parents

p105

A

Let's Play!

What do you do on Saturdays, Eva?

I play ball with Jenny.

Who's Jenny?

She's my cousin.

Where do you play?

We play at the park.

Then what do you do?

We have pizza with my uncle. Then, we play with dolls. How about you, Jay?

I swim, and I fly my kite.

That's nice!

C

See script of *Let's Play!*.

p106

D

1. My grandparents go to the store.
2. My cousin likes plums.
3. My uncle has a red car.

p107

A

Annie and the Toy

Annie is in bed. She looks for Teddy Bear. Teddy Bear has a blue vest. Where is he?

Annie looks under the bed.

"He isn't here."

Annie looks at the bike. She sees a blue vest. It's Teddy Bear. "He's here!"

Annie is in bed. She's happy.

"I like my teddy bear," says Annie.

C

See script of *Annie and the Toy*.

p108

D

1. bike
2. boat
3. scooter
4. teddy bear

p109

A

A Rainy Day

"Look at the rain!" says Eric. "I can't go to the park! I don't like rain!"

Eric is hungry. He finds some food.

"I like tomato juice, but I don't like tomatoes." "I like carrot cake, but I don't like carrots."

Eric eats cake. He plays video games.

"Today is a fun day!" says Eric.

C

See script of *A Rainy Day*.

p110

D

1. "I want a tomato," says Rita.
2. He puts the mango in the box.
3. We get carrots at the store.

p111

A

The Sisters

Three girls live in the blue house.

Kay is the tall sister. She has long legs. She can jump!

Fran is the short sister. She has red hair. She can sing!

Ella is the baby. She has a little body. She can stamp!

Fran sings. Kay jumps. Ella stamps. The cat runs!

Stop, girls, stop!

C

See script of *The Sisters*.

p112

D

1. legs
2. head
3. body
4. teeth

p113

A

The Acrobat

Hello, Pierre. What can you do?

Hello, Henri. I can walk on my hands.

Oh.

I can make a T with my body. Look!

Oh!

I can touch my eyes with my feet. I can touch my nose, too.

Stop there, Pierre! Can I take a picture?

Yes, Henri!

Smile! That's great! Thank you!

C

See script of *The Acrobat*.

p114

D

1. I can touch my face.
2. This is my nose.
3. She has pretty eyes.